A2 GOVERNMENT & POLITICS:
IDEOLOGIES &
IDEOLOGIES IN ACTION

TEXTBO   VISION GUIDE AND EXAM GUIDE

DUNCA

© Peel Island Productions, 2011

Skipton, Yorkshire

UK

http://peelisland.blogspot.com

ISBN: 978-1-4477-3399-7

Acknowledgements

Thanks to Julia Hall, Brian Hall, Steve Cartman, Nick Hall, Jonathan Smith and Virginia Hall for encouragement, proof-reading, etc. Any mistakes in this book are most definitely my own, but I am indebted to them and others for their assistance. Even the A2 Government & Politics class of 2011/12 (Aaron, Charles, Hannah, Josh, Nathan and Peter) deserve a mention for having spotted some dreadful typos in the Liberalism glossary!! I would also like to thank all the Government and Politics students who have ever studied either of these modules with me, as no doubt some of your collective wisdom has rubbed off along the way.

CONTENTS

INTRODUCTION   7

PART ONE: IDEOLOGIES   9

1. INTRODUCTION TO IDEOLOGIES   9

2. LIBERALISM   13
   a. Historical context   13
   b. Varieties of liberalism   16
   c. Liberalism and contemporary party politics   23
   d. Answering exam questions on liberalism   30
   e. Liberalism glossary   35

3. SOCIALISM   38
   a. Historical context   38
   b. Varieties of socialism   45
   c. Socialism and contemporary party politics   49
   d. Answering exam questions on socialism   53
   e. Socialism glossary   56

4. CONSERVATISM   59
   a. Historical context   59
   b. Varieties of conservatism   63
   c. Conservatism and contemporary party   67
      politics
   d. Answering exam questions on   70
      conservatism
   e. Conservatism glossary   73

5. FASCISM   75
   a. Historical context   75

b. Varieties of fascism 79

c. Fascism and contemporary politics 80

d. Answering exam questions on fascism 85

e. Fascism glossary 88

PART TWO: POLITICAL ISSUES - IDEOLOGIES IN ACTION 90

1. ETHNICITY & GENDER 91

a. Key issues 91

  i. Ethnicity

  ii. Gender

b. Key legislation and reform 100

c. Ethnicity, gender and contemporary party politics 101

d. Answering exam questions on Ethnicity and Gender 101

e. Ethnicity and gender glossary 104

2. EDUCATION 106

a. Key issues 106

b. Key legislation and reform 114

c. Education and contemporary party politics 123

d. Answering exam questions on Education 125

e. Education glossary 126

3. ECONOMY 128

a. Key issues 128

b. Key developments 133

c. Contemporary party politics and Economics 135

d. Answering exam questions on the Economy 135

e. Economy glossary   *138*

4. THE ENVIRONMENT   *140*

    a. Key issues   *140*

    b. The Environment and contemporary   *144*
       party and pressure group politics

    c. Answering exam questions on The   *147*
       Environment

    d. Environment glossary   *150*

PART THREE: REVISION AND EXAM   *152*
TECHNIQUES AND TOP TIPS
SELECT BIBLIOGRAPHY AND RECOMMENDED   *156*
FURTHER READING
MODEL ANSWER PLANS   *157*

INTRODUCTION

This book should be seen as a launch-pad: it is not intended to be a detailed and comprehensive account of everything that could possibly be referred to in answers in these modules. Rather this book should give the student a grounding in the fundamentals of the relevant modules, alongside signposts towards further detail, amplification and up-to-date examples to use. This book is not designed to take up a lot of shelf room and be a rarely-read safety blanket for an anxious student, rather it is intended to be *useful*: a practical guide to doing well in A2 Government and Politics. As such, you will be guided through the content in easy-to-follow steps, where material can be displayed or summarised in tables or diagrams it will be, where technical terms are used you will be able to find them in a glossary and exam hints play a central part throughout the book. *Synoptic links* will also be pointed out, where material learnt in AS Government & Politics can prove invaluable at A2.

A lot of students study the US Politics modules at A2 but if you are one of the lucky students whose college or school has chosen to focus on ideologies, you are in for a treat. The ideology modules are what many students hope Politics is going to be like when they first sign up for it, and they provide a base of knowledge that will be invaluable for those students who hope to take up Politics in higher education.

Students who study History, Philosophy or Sociology alongside Government and Politics will find plenty of opportunities to use transferrable knowledge between their subjects. Politics students should not be scared of philosophy, history or theory: these are the tools with which we can understand contemporary politics.

This book is written primarily with the AQA specification in mind, but will also be of use for students with all the main UK exam boards.

To accompany the book there is a website that has all of the links referred to in the text and also "blog" updates regarding relevant news.

http://a2ideologies.blogspot.com

Do make use of this website, as politics never stops and so a book can never be 100% up-to-date.

Exam-style questions and model answers in this book are based on the style of AQA exam questions and related directly to the specification; however, should any be the same as past or future exam papers, specimen papers or mark schemes, this is entirely coincidental.

PART ONE: IDEOLOGIES

INTRODUCTION TO IDEOLOGIES

In the context of this module, we are using the term "Ideology" to mean a particular broad set of ideas about politics. The four "ideologies" considered are: Liberalism, Socialism, Conservatism and Fascism. This is different from the Marxist concept of ideology (that some students might have encountered in Sociology, for example) – i.e. the set of ideas put forward by the ruling class to disguise their exploitation of the workers. Don't forget that Marxist concept altogether (it will prove rather useful when *evaluating* these ideologies) but don't be distracted by it either! However, it is important to remember some ideologies are themselves quite opposed to ideology, defining themselves as *pragmatic* and, as such, *non-ideological* (e.g. traditional conservatism).

The ideologies we will consider are *so* broad that disagreements within them are often more hostile than disagreements between the ideologies. Therefore, the focus in the following sections will often be on the different traditions within the ideologies in question.

At various points throughout AS Government and Politics, reference will have been made to the concepts of "left", "right" and "centre" and, when considering political parties, there will have been some investigation of "socialism" and "conservatism" and even "New Right" or "neo-liberalism". But it is undoubtedly an area that some people get stuck on or find confusing.

This is not really surprising! It is far from straightforward. Many people today use the term "liberal" in the modern US sense of "left-wing", while simultaneously talking about the "liberal" economic policies of right-wing governments. Individuals with such different views as Tony Blair, Tony Benn, Saddam Hussain and Joseph Stalin might all have been described by themselves or others as "socialist", while "fascist" has come to be used as a fairly general term of abuse without necessarily any political connection at all!

Left / Right

Political ideology is often described as a spectrum, with socialist views on the left and conservative views on the right. For mainstream British party politics, such an approach is quite effective. We can follow the spectrum from the "Labour left" or "hard left" (e.g. the Socialist Campaign Group of Labour MPs), through mainstream Labour (centre left), "New Labour" and most Liberal Democrats (centre), through a spectrum of centre-right and right-wing politics represented by the Conservative Party and small parties to their right.

LINK TO AS : THE POLITICAL CENTRE

Why has mainstream politics in the UK become so crowded in the middle? Labour, Conservative and – of course – the Liberal Democrats have all rushed to the centre-ground of political ideology and, as such, have become "catch all" parties – trying to get voters of all classes and with a wide range of conflicting interests. They clearly see this as the most effective way to get elected. They focus on the "median" voter (in 1997 this was the much talked about "Mondeo Man") who is seen as the key to *marginal seats*. What happens if political parties take their *core vote* for granted or entirely abandon their traditional ideological perspective?

At AS you had to explain terms for 5 marks. Revisit this skill by explaining the following terms:

"Catch all" parties

Marginal seats

Core vote

This will serve as useful revision and encourage you to be *synoptic* in your approach to A2 Government and Politics

---

The left-right spectrum becomes more problematic if we try and define quite what the features of "left wing" and "right wing" politics are.

One approach is to focus on how left-wing politics tend to be *collective* and right-wing politics more *individualistic*. This makes sense when comparing traditional socialism with perhaps the politics of Margaret Thatcher. A related approach would be to see left-wing politics as involving a strong role for the state and right-wing politics as leaving things to the free market. However, most people would consider anarchist politics (which sees *no* role for the state) as *left wing* and fascism (which proposes a very active role for the state) as *right wing*.

Another approach is to focus on *authoritarianism*. This approach sees right-wing politics as being authoritarian and hierarchical while left-wing politics are radical and "bottom up", championing people's freedom and rights. While this might work for the right-wing politics of Adolf Hitler and the left-wing approach of Nelson Mandela, it fails to explain how Joseph Stalin might be described as left wing.

As such, the terms "left" and "right" must always be treated with caution and come alongside some further explanation and context. It also explains why people continue to try and find alternative ways of explaining people's political perspectives.

ACTIVITY: THE POLITICAL COMPASS

Go to http://www.politicalcompass.org/ and answer the detailed questionnaire about political views found there. This will plot your position on a four-point "political compass" and you can compare yourself with well-known political figures from around the world. **How does this differ from a left-right spectrum?**

As we work through the four ideologies included in this book, the relationships between them will be considered in some detail. Each ideology is a separate "topic" on your exam paper, but really they cannot be seen in isolation. For example, traditional conservatism cannot really be understood without considering it as a response to liberal ideas.

In the exam itself, you will choose two topics (ideologies) from the four. There is a lot to be said for having the broadest possible choice of questions in the exam; however some students do choose to focus on three of the topics instead of all four, allowing some choice but enabling more targeted revision.

A2 assessment usually requires the student to be *synoptic* and these modules are no different. The exam boards want to see evidence of making connections between the various different aspects of the whole two-year specification. The section on Political

Parties from the first AS module provides most of the opportunities to be "synoptic" in the Ideologies module as the exam questions tend to link ideologies to contemporary party politics.

Understanding political ideology is a key to a much greater understanding of politics more generally. Let's make a start!

LIBERALISM

A. Historical context

Today "liberal" is a widely used and misused term. In the US it is often used as a term of abuse for those who tend towards the Democrat left (ironic, in a nation founded on the liberal ideology). In the UK it is often used to mean "moderate", "middle-of-the-road" or "centrist" although it is also used to mean "progressive". However, liberalism can only properly be understood in its historical context. Despite its modern-day association with gradualist reform and political moderation, liberalism has a bloody and revolutionary history.

Liberalism has its roots in *the Enlightenment* – the Age of Reason, where science, logic and rationalism challenged the supernatural ideology of the medieval period. For centuries, politics across Europe was based on ideas of hereditary hierarchy: some were born to rule, others born to be ruled. This hierarchy was based on the idea that the King had a *divine right* to rule, and that there was a divine chain of being: one's place in the hierarchy was God's will; dissent and even aspiration were therefore against the will of God. However, at various points in history people with power and influence have chosen to question the *ideology* of the Divine Right of Kings. In medieval society, it was the aristocracy who sought a greater role for themselves (made law in the UK through the Magna Carta), but in the early modern period and particularly through the eras of industrialisation, a new class acquired wealth and status in European society, a class that was denied power or influence in the still largely feudal political systems that dominated Europe. This was a class of "commoners" who earned money. They were traders and business people, originating from the "middling sorts" of society who, in an age of exploration and foreign trade, could make vast sums of money. This was the class that Karl Marx called "the bourgeoisie", the owners of the means of production. And it was from this class that serious challenges to the concepts of divine right and hereditary power emerged across Europe, bringing with it reform or revolution (and reaction on the part of the *ancien regimes* that the liberals sought to topple).

This serious challenge came to be known as liberalism and from its earliest roots included a notion of equality – that "all men are born equal". (Although "men" is used as a generic term for "human being" there was little appetite for women's rights among the early liberals). From the beginnings of liberalism there was also a strong concept of *rights*. People had rights, either "natural" or "human rights" that everyone is born with, or else "civil rights" that go hand in hand with being a *citizen*. Those who are expected to pay taxes, for example, should have civil rights (e.g. the right to vote) that go along with that civic responsibility. This then was the other basic tenet of early liberalism: a notion of social contract or constitutional settlement where people's rights and responsibilities were enshrined in law.

This revolutionary ideology was expressed in the simple slogan of the French Revolution: "liberté, egalité, fraternité!" (Freedom, Equality and brotherhood!)

Philosophical influences on this revolutionary creed included Thomas Paine (*The Rights of Man)* and Jean-Jacques Rousseau (*The Social Contract)*. The French Revolution triggered a great many European revolutions as well as what would perhaps become the most significant revolution of all: the American War of Independence.

Even in the UK, which had its revolution in the 17th century and was considered the "Mother of Parliaments", political life was not immune to the liberal contagion. While, for the most part, the calls for reform were able to be expressed through the Whig Party in Parliament, radical meetings were roughly dispersed (famously and bloodily at the "Peterloo Massacre" in Manchester in 1819) and the Chartist movement grew rapidly, calling for much greater and more fundamental reform than was being offered by Whig governments.

Key to these reforms was the extension of the *franchise*. Even in the UK, that had enjoyed a form of parliamentary democracy for more than 100 years before the French Revolution, there was little or no real democracy at all. A tiny proportion of the population were entitled to vote, the sizes of parliamentary divisions or boroughs varied widely and the elected House of Commons was just one part of a sovereign Parliament that also included the hereditary House of Lords and Monarch. Only the most radical of radical liberals dared challenge the UK's constitutional monarchy; instead calls for reform focused on allowing more groups in society to be allowed to vote. The rallying cry was "universal manhood suffrage"; the reality was a slow process of reform in which an increasing number of men were entitled to vote.

Although Marx would describe such events as the French Revolution and the American War of Independence as "bourgeois revolutions", surely the liberal demands of equality, human rights, universal suffrage and an end to inherited privilege would benefit all, not just this new powerful industrialist class?

The *universality* of early liberalism can certainly be challenged. "Universal Manhood Suffrage" did not include women, of course, but nor did it include slaves in the new United States of America. The slaves were not protected by the Bill of Rights, either. Further, while democracy was yearned for, this was not to be mistaken for "populism"; the US Constitution involved many checks and balances to avoid "the tyranny of the majority". One of these checks to "mob rule" was to have the President elected indirectly, via an electoral college. While all men were born equal, some were more capable of making sensible and responsible decisions than others!

One of the most important rights that early liberals defended was that of *private property*, which was clearly more of a pressing issue to those who owned some (and this was a small minority). The concern about private property extended to taxation, therefore early liberals wanted to be sure that rates were not spent in a rash or wasteful way. As such, in the UK, it was classical liberals who were the great champions of the New Poor Laws of the 1820s, that gave the poor as meagre relief as possible in the workhouses. Liberal thinker, Thomas Malthus, believed that poor relief encouraged the poor to breed, worsening the problem, while another liberal, Jeremy Bentham, felt that the happiness of the rate payer should take precedence over the happiness of the very poor minority.

Liberals wanted to protect citizens from the state, and saw no role for the state in protecting some citizens from others. Some of the most passionate defenders of the slave trade were liberals. They saw a ban, or even regulation, as the state interfering in the free market. What an individual wishes to do with his property is a matter for the individual, and that includes human beings. A similar approach was taken in relation to working hours and child labour: Liberals fought for the status quo while a small army of traditional, paternalistic Tories led the calls for reform.

The approach many liberals took to poor relief, slavery and workers' rights makes the Marxist charge of this being "just ideology" (i.e. a false set of ideas designed to justify and normalise power and exploitation) more compelling (although, of course, the same charge could be levelled at Marxism itself, in many 20th century regimes). However, it would be wrong to tar all 19th century liberals with the same brush.

There were "progressive liberals", like John Stuart Mill, and many radicals, whose natural inclinations were towards championing the rights and interests of the least well off in society. The roots of social or "positive" liberalism (discussed in the next section) can be traced to these progressives and radicals.

B. Varieties of liberalism

There is not just one liberalism, but many liberalisms. What we have discussed so far, in the previous section, is *classical liberalism*. This was that dangerous idea that sparked so many revolutions: that people were equal, that the state should leave people alone (people should be allowed to be free), and that if the state made demands of its citizens, it also had to grant them rights, in a social contract.

Key liberal thinkers include the aforementioned Thomas Paine, Jean-Jacques Rousseau and Jeremy Bentham. At the conclusion of the section on the historical context, I mentioned the progressive Liberal MP, John Stuart Mill, whose essay "On Liberty" is considered to be a clear explanation of the broad liberal philosophy.

Mill argued that people should be free to do what they like, so long as in doing so they do not restrict the freedom of others.

This helps explain the concept of *absolute rights* and *qualified rights*. Some rights should be available to all citizens (e.g. the right to vote; there is no caveat that you must vote responsibly – people can spoil their ballot papers, vote for novelty candidates or fascists, etc.) while other rights are *qualified*, e.g. "the right to free speech". There are various restrictions on free speech. An example that is often used is that we have a right to free speech, but we don't have the right to shout "fire!" in a crowded room: we are expected to use our right to free speech responsibly. One way of explaining this could be that the irresponsible use of our free speech might restrict somebody else's freedom (e,g. their freedom not to be discriminated against).

Another key liberal thinker was Adam Smith, who concentrated on a very important aspect of classical liberalism: economic freedom. Adam Smith believed that the state should have a very limited role in economics and that the best decisions and best outcomes would be reached by "the invisible hand of the market". The principle that emerges from this view is *laissez-faire*. This means that the government should "leave it be" when it comes to economic policy. It is this *economic* aspect of classical liberalism that has had perhaps the most impact on modern UK politics, ironically through the policies of a right-wing *conservative* Prime Minister, Margaret Thatcher. Her enthusiasm for "neo-liberalism" was hugely influential across all three of the main political parties in the UK. However, laissez-faire economics found its way into conservative ideology before the arrival of Thatcher, as we shall see in part four.

Our next variety of liberalism is given many names. You might hear it described as "New Liberalism", "social liberalism", "welfare liberalism" or "positive liberalism" and, while its roots lie in the progressive views of people like John Stuart Mill, it is the Liberal governments of the early 20th century that are most associated with the concept.

In 1906, the Liberal Party swept to a landslide victory, exacting a punishing defeat on the Conservative Party. In the same year, the Labour Representation Committee formally turned itself into the Labour Party, a move that would ultimately condemn the Liberal Party to third party status. It is possible that the threat from the nascent Labour Party had an impact on changes in the thinking of the Liberal Party. The influence of "Lib-Lab" MPs around the turn of the century might also have played its part. What was this big change? The Liberal Party began to see an active role for the state. This role centred around the concept of *positive freedom*.

Liberals concerned with positive freedom considered the notion of freedom or liberty at the heart of classical liberalism to be rather *negative*. It was all about defending people from a state that tried to prevent them from doing things. Surely liberty was also about setting people free? *Enabling* people to do things! Surely this was a legitimate role for the state. A classical liberal approach to welfare, for example, could be seen as pushing for people to have the freedom to starve.

From this perspective, what could be illiberal about compulsory education, free school meals or an old age pension?

DEBATE: TWO TYPES OF FREEOM

There's a challenge for you! What *could* be illiberal about compulsory education, free school meals or an old age pension? Divide your group into classical, economic liberals and New Liberals and debate it!

The answer of course, from a "laissez-faire" economic liberal perspective, is quite a lot! All of it discourages *self-help* and encourages idleness and dependency! Free school meals reward lazy and feckless parents, saving them money; old age pensions (even those based entirely on a state-administered insurance policy) involve *coercion* -- individuals should have the right to save or not to save, and those who choose the former should reap the rewards.

Between 1906 and the First World War, Liberal politicians engaged in quite a radical period of reform, in many ways planting the seeds of the Welfare State that would lie largely dormant for a further thirty years. They met fierce resistance from the Conservative Party, not least in the House of Lords where they had a permanent in-built majority. This led to significant reform of the House of Lords in the Parliament Act of 1911. As such, as well as their association with pro-welfare policies, the New Liberals are also associated with radical constitutional reform. However, David Lloyd George is also now famous for having sold seats in the House of the Lords which rather undermines the democratic credentials of the great constitutional reformer.

The long-term impact of social liberalism as an idea might well have benefited the Labour Party more than the Liberal Party. It is worth bearing in mind that the two academics whose ideas were to have the greatest influence on economic and social policy following the Second World War, and particularly during the 1945-51 Labour government, were John Maynard Keynes and William Beveridge, both of them Liberals.

The "strange death of Liberal England" meant that, after Lloyd George, the Liberal Party was really confined to the margins of UK Politics. But liberalism as an ideology remained very much at the centre of things. The social liberalism of the Lloyd-George period had much in common with the rather moderate, English form of socialism promoted by the mainstream of the Labour Party, while the economic aspects of classical liberalism found great champions in the Conservative Party.

In Part Three, we consider socialism and, in doing so, we will look in detail at the political ideas known as "social democracy". The differences between social liberalism and social democracy are very slight, allowing for quite a comfortable merging of the Liberal Party and the Social Democratic Party in the 1980s to form the Liberal Democrats.

In Part Four, we consider the New Right of conservatism, with its "neo-liberal" economic outlook, as well as the contribution of *libertarian* thinkers to modern conservative ideology.

At the start of the 21st century, we had an interesting twist in the liberal tale. A number of young Liberal Democrats (including future government ministers like Nick Clegg, David Laws and Danny Alexander) became known as the "orange book" liberals. These "orange book" liberals were keen to return the focus of Liberal Democrats to their *liberal* half, and away from the social democracy that had, in the 1990s, led to the Liberal Democrats finding themselves in the unlikely position of being seen by many as being the party of the left in the UK! The "orange book" liberals were influenced by their classical liberal forefathers and felt that the late 20th century Liberal Democrat Party was too dismissive of "public sector reform", market forces and a greater role for the private sector.

This "right turn" in the Liberal Democrat thinking was given a vote of confidence by party members when they chose Nick Clegg as their leader, and paved the way for the Liberal Democrat Party to be able to form a coherent coalition government with the Conservative Party in 2010.

What could be more *liberal* (classically liberal) than the idea of the Big Society?

Nick Clegg – Liberal Democrat Leader

THE BIG SOCIETY: LIBERALISM IN GOVERNMENT?

Go online and read
http://www.conservatives.com/News/Speeches/2009/11/David_Cameron_The_Big_Society.aspx

where David Cameron explains what he means by the Big Society. Use *liberal* arguments to both support *and* criticise the Big Society as a political idea.

C. Liberalism and contemporary party politics

Which of the modern UK political parties are the true inheritors of liberalism? Let's consider each in turn:

The Labour Party

Tony Blair publically regretted what he described as a "schism" in "progressive" politics in the early 20th century. While this worried some Labour Party members (as by regretting that "schism" he was effectively regretting the founding of the Labour Party!) it shows that, for Blair at any rate, liberal politics were progressive politics, and the Labour and Liberal parties were essentially in the same business. But how *liberal* was the last Labour government?

The last Labour government was *proactive* in challenging discrimination and promoting rights. By introducing the Disability Discrimination Act, the Human Rights Act, legislation protecting individuals from racial and religious hatred and, ultimately, the Equality Act, a clear argument can be made to say that Labour took their liberal principles of equality and rights very seriously.

Of course, some liberals could take a very different view, seeing much of the anti-discrimination, pro-rights legislation as encumbering business with red tape and regulation, therefore interfering with the proper workings of the free market. Some liberals might also point to restrictions on the freedom of speech, particularly in relation to the laws on incitement of racial and religious hatred.

If we are to see democratic and constitutional reform as key elements of liberalism, then there is also much to comment on. New Labour in government removed most of the hereditary peers from the House of Lords and introduced a more independent approach to the creation of new peers (though the job of reforming the House of Lords was left very much unfinished when they left office in 2010). New Labour devolved power to executives and legislatures in Scotland, Wales, Northern Ireland and London and began a process of allowing the English regions to decide through referenda whether they wanted devolution too. The Labour government also introduced a Freedom of Information Act to allow individuals greater access to personal information held about them.

However, some of this constitutional reform was unfinished or unconvincing. Devolution may have benefited those living in the areas with devolved assemblies, but some would argue that it has not been organised and consistent enough to make constitutional sense. If writing a constitution for the UK, it is unlikely anybody would arrive at the current situation (especially relating to devolution and the House of Lords) by design.

ACTIVITY: A CODIFIED CONSTITUTION FOR THE UK

If *you* were writing a new constitution for the UK how would you resolve questions like devolution and the second chamber? Would you have an all-elected House of Lords? Would you have an English Parliament, or parliaments for the English regions? Do you agree that it is unlikely that anybody would arrive at our current constitution by design?

Try writing a brief overview of a UK constitution on a single sheet of paper. How does your design differ from the constitution we actually have?

Furthermore, the Labour Party in government disappointed many constitutional reformers because they did not change the voting system. In the 1997 General Election campaign, Labour promised a report into proportional representation followed by a referendum. The report took place, chaired by Roy Jenkins, and it proposed a system called AV+ (a form of hybrid, Additional Member System). No referendum was ever held.

From a social liberal perspective, the Labour government could also be applauded for moves such as the minimum wage, paid paternity leave and "compensatory education schemes" such as Surestart.

However, from an economic liberal perspective, the minimum wage is a serious intervention in the market, coercing employers to pay people more than they believe them to be worth. Paid paternity leave is, again, more red tape and cost for the employer, and Surestart centres have to be paid for and those who pay the highest taxes are those least likely to make use of them.

From an economic liberal perspective, the 1997-2010 Labour governments could be praised, at least until the last year or so of their government, for maintaining many of the neo-liberal assumptions about the economy that characterised the preceding

Conservative years. New Labour did not reverse any Conservative privatisations (and indeed added some of their own, including Air Traffic Control) and did not reverse any of the restrictions on Trade Union activities introduced by the Thatcher government. New Labour also introduced private finance and market principles into the public sector through the Private Finance Initiative and a range of "part privatisations". While social liberals would tend to oppose this approach, economic liberals would find little to fault. However, the Labour government's response to the credit crunch and global recession from the late 2000s was certainly not in the neo-liberal tradition, preferring a more Keynesian approach (see later section on the Economy).

The Labour governments of 1997-2010 also introduced some measures that might clearly be described as *illiberal*, most of them in the arena of the criminal justice system and many after 2001 as part of the War on Terror. There was the removal of "double jeopardy" (not being able to be tried for the same crime more than once), a reduction in the use of trial by jury, increases in the amount of time suspects can be held without charge and a real, concerted effort to introduce compulsory ID cards. All forms of liberalism would be critical of these measures. You might well be able to come up with all sorts of justifications for them, and that is an important point to remember: There is a powerful liberal hegemony in the Western world today (meaning that liberal ideas have, for the most part, become "common sense") but the most liberal take on something is not necessarily the most correct!

ACTIVITY: LABOUR PARTY POLICY TODAY

Go onto the Labour Party's website (http://www.labour.org.uk) and find a handful of their current, bang up-to-date policies. On no more than one sheet of A4 for each policy, analyse them in terms of their *liberalism* as above. Remember to consider whether *all* liberals would approve or disapprove of the policy in question and why.

It is a good idea to keep a file specifically relating to policies and case studies: this activity (and the several similar ones you will find in this section and similar sections throughout the book) will help you produce this file.

The Conservative Party

Although the roots of conservatism stem from a fear of liberalism, there is quite a strong case to be made for the modern Conservative Party to be the real heirs of the liberal ideology in UK party politics today. The area where this is most apparent is in terms of economic policy where the Conservative Party has whole-heartedly embraced a "neo-liberal" approach.

Gordon Brown labelled the Conservative Party the "do nothing" party during the credit crunch and global recession of the late 2000s as they opposed many of Brown's policies for "bailing out" the banks and investing in training and job creation. Whether or not the charge was entirely fair, classical economic liberals would, indeed, propose a "laissez-faire" approach. If not exactly a "do nothing" strategy, it could certainly be viewed as a strategy that concludes that the solutions to economic problems will not be provided by the state. Cutting red tape and regulation, encouraging entrepreneurship and allowing the market to work would be the policies of classic economic liberals and is broadly the approach of George Osborne and the modern Conservative Party. Furthermore, the deep cuts in public spending in which the Conservative-led government is engaging are also consistent with a classic economic liberal approach. A large public sector interferes with the free market. Furthermore, public services cost the tax-payer money. Those people who pay the most taxes (the better off) are those who have the least occasion to use the public services. From this perspective, classic economic liberals would argue that, at the very least, government should ensure that taxpayers are getting value for money and no money is wasted or defrauded. They would further argue that, if a private company or other private body could provide those services more cheaply or, preferably, at no cost, then they should always be preferred.

David Cameron's big idea of the Big Society perfectly fits into this neo-liberal approach. It is a small state, low tax, pro-self help approach to public service. It is classically liberal.

However, social liberals would question the real impact of these policies on individuals. They would argue that the laissez-faire approach to economic crisis was one that inevitably involved high unemployment. The liberal (but decidedly not neo-liberal) economist Keynes argued that the main aim of macro-economic policy should be to promote full employment. Cameron and Osborne's main aim is, they argue, to balance the books. Social liberals would be particularly concerned about the human cost of the cuts. The services that are *easiest* to cut are those that benefit minorities and groups with little power or influence in society and, while Bentham and the utilitarians could certainly make a liberal case for cutting such services, it is just such people who require setting free. It is their rights and interests that the state needs to promote, for they are not in a position to promote them for themselves. Social liberals would also look here for the limits of the Big Society. To "do it yourself" you require time and resources, and these are things that are very ill-distributed in our society. Those with money and leisure are in a much stronger position to build the Big Society than those who are over-worked and underpaid, and this is of particular concern to social liberals. Social liberals would also point to the impact of the cuts on certain groups, such as students. The trebling of tuition fees would be a definite concern for social liberals, while economic liberals would see this policy as being, essentially, the privatisation and marketisation of the university system, and therefore a good thing.

There are other ways in which the Conservative Party appears to have inherited the mantle of liberalism. In the 1980s, the Conservative Party's neo-liberalism appeared to be very much reserved to the economic arena. The Conservative Party of the 1980s responded to the Northern Ireland "troubles" in a similarly "illiberal" way to the Labour government's reactions to Islamist terrorism: the use of internment, etc. The Conservative Party was also accused of being "illiberal" in the way it policed strikes and riots, and the domestic political use it made of the security services in relation to radical groups and trade unions. But the Conservative Party of the 2000s, when it was in opposition, took a much more liberal approach to law and order and domestic security matters. When David Davies was Shadow Home Secretary, the Conservatives fought "illiberal" anti-terror laws particularly strongly and Davies eventually left the front bench to fight an ill-advised by-election on the single issue of ID cards.

In Government, the Conservatives have been less clearly *liberal* in this area, despite being in coalition with the Liberal Democrats. While the ID card scheme has been abandoned, that could be put down as much to being a victim of the cuts as to being an active *liberal* act. At the time of writing there have been no attempts to reduce the amount of time suspects can be held without trial or otherwise reverse any of the last Labour government's anti-terror measures. Furthermore, the way that student protests and anti-cuts protests have been policed has been criticised in similar terms to those used in the 1980s. Following the August riots in 2011, David Cameron and other conservatives promoted a number of "illiberal" responses, including considering the use of plastic bullets and water canon and bringing in the army.

The Liberal Democrats

Of course, the Liberal Democrats are the modern-day Liberal Party and would
certainly claim to be the true liberal party in modern UK Politics. But what kind of
liberalism do they now represent?

As previously mentioned, the Liberal Democrat Party (with its origins in the merger
of the old Liberal Party and the Social Democratic Party, who had split from the
Labour Party in the early 1980s) has been assuredly *social* liberal, rejecting the
laissez-faire approach of the neo-liberals in the Conservative Party and what it saw
as the more socialist policies of Labour in the 80s. Through the 90s and 2000s, with
the rightward lurch of Labour under Blair, the Liberal Democrats came to be seen by
many as being to the left of Labour. While the party was on safe liberal territory on
issues of constitutional change (strongly promoting changing the voting system to
proportional representation and championing a wholly-elected second chamber) and
on law, order and domestic security (opposing what it saw as illegitimate increases
in state power) it maintained a social democratic attachment to public services, the
NHS, comprehensive education, free higher education, etc. This could all be
interpreted as social liberalism. In being the only mainstream party to oppose the
Iraq War and, at times, having an anti-nuclear stance, the party seemed to be
occupying a more traditional left-wing position, one abandoned by the Labour
Party.

However, as part of the Con-Dem coalition government, the Liberal Democrats have
rediscovered economic liberalism. And, as previously discussed, this is not just
about the pragmatic realities of being the junior partner in a coalition: the "orange
book" liberals had already set out to reclaim official Liberalism from the Social
Democrats.

MINDMAP: LIBERALISM TODAY

On a single sheet of paper (a big one!), construct a mindmap using all the phrases, terms, people, policies, etc. listed here. Make your own connections. Again, you may need to go beyond this chapter and this book to make all these connections.

Tony Blair	David Cameron
Third Way	The Big Society
Progressive	Neo-liberalism
New Right	Human Rights Act
Equality Act	Social Liberalism
Economic Liberalism	"Orange Book" Liberalism
Nick Clegg	Tuition Fees
Alternative Vote	Proportional Representation
Roy Jenkins	George Osborne
Budget Cuts	ID cards
David Davies	Detention Without Trial
Minimum Wage	Laissez-Faire
Margaret Thatcher	Gordon Brown
Keynes	Friedman

When you have made all the connections, start adding your own branches with further ideas. This will prove a useful document for revision. (You could also use *prezi.com*)

D. Answering exam questions on liberalism

On the AQA exam paper there will be two questions on the Liberalism topic. If you choose Liberalism as one of your two topics, you must answer both questions. There will be a ten mark question and a thirty mark question.

The Ten Mark Question

Remember the five mark question from AS? You were asked to explain a term as used in an extract. There are no extracts on the A2 paper, but terminology is still at the heart of this question. If the five mark question could be described as a "definition plus" question, the ten mark question asks for a little bit more, usually either a contextualisation or a compare and contrast.

EXAMPLE ONE

Topic 1: Liberalism

01   Explain the difference between *civil rights* and *human rights* (10 marks)

This is an example of a *compare and contrast* 10 mark question. A good answer to this question would give a comprehensive explanation of both terms, but an outstanding answer would focus on how they differed, illustrated by examples. In other words, for 10 marks, a detailed explanation is really required.

Your marks are divided up into A01, A02 and A03 marks. A01 is Knowledge and Understanding, A02 Analysis and Evaluation and A03 Communication. To get the A01 marks for the above question, you need an accurate and detailed definition of both terms. Any examples should be accurate and relevant. Comparing, contrasting and contextualisng will give you the A02 marks, while a good level of English and the proper use of correct political terminology will bring you the A03 marks.

Let's try and nail the A01 marks first of all.

The concept of *rights* is at the heart of liberalism. One important set of rights that people should enjoy are *human rights* or *natural rights*. These are rights that all humans should share. The United Nations Declaration of Human Rights and the European Convention on Human Rights have set out to codify these natural rights, including the right to life, freedom of expression, freedom of assembly, etc. Civil rights, on the other hand are rights that people enjoy as citizens of a particular nation-state, as part of a social contract. Citizenship bestows certain rights upon individuals and these go hand in hand with the *responsibilities* of citizenship (e.g. paying taxes, obeying the law, etc.) These rights might include the right to vote. The Bill of Rights in the US Constitution is an example of a list of civil rights (although some of the rights included therein might equally be considered human rights).

So far, so good. The two types of rights have been carefully explained and illustrated with relevant examples. In doing this, correct terminology has been used, so AO3 marks have been accumulated too. Defining the two terms together does go *some* way to explaining the difference but there is certainly an opportunity to acquire some more AO2 marks.

The key difference between civil rights and human rights is that civil rights are those that we only enjoy because of our citizenship. For example, a US citizen could not vote in a UK general election without holding dual citizenship. However, that US citizen living in the UK would, of course, still have the right to life and free speech, etc: these are human rights. Most things that we would consider human rights might also be listed among civil rights (although the US constitution does not guarantee the right to life) but there are certainly examples of civil rights that would not be considered human rights. In the US, for example, citizens have the right to "bear arms".

You should aim for a comprehensive, detailed response like this.

EXAMPLE TWO:

Topic 1: Liberalism

01   Why are liberals champions of constitutional reform?

This is a *contextualisation* question. It clearly would not be enough to explain the term *constitutional reform*. The key word here is *why*. What is it about the ideology of liberalism that leads its followers to want to make constitutional reforms? A01 marks will come both from an explanation of what is meant by constitutional reform, but also by accurately identifying the relevant elements of the liberal ideology that directly relate to this. A02 marks come from putting these together, but also perhaps from some debate. Are all liberals champions of constitutional reform? Are there any non-ideological reasons why liberals might champion it? Let's have a look at it:

Liberalism is an ideology about the relationship between the state and the individual. That relationship is governed by constitutions. Jean-Jacques Rousseau, in his work *The Social Contract* developed the idea that citizens have rights and responsibilities. Liberals see a constitution as an important guarantor of rights and, perhaps most importantly, as something that *limits* the power of the state. Without a clear set of rules, a state might demand too much of its citizens, or it might unfairly restrict their freedom.

Constitutional reform is a broad term to refer to any change to a constitution, but is understood to mean making that constitution more democratic and more representative. In the UK, this might mean reforming those parts of the constitution that are hereditary (the Crown) or appointed (the House of Lords), bringing government and representation closer to the people (devolution) and improving the representativeness of representative bodies (electoral reform). It might also mean opting for a *codified* constitution.

For liberals, it is only a democratic mandate that gives the state any legitimate authority, and therefore it is essential that the state is as democratic as possible.

However, *economic* liberals do not appear to have been overly concerned about constitutional reform. Furthermore, the modern-day Liberal Democrat Party might have more pragmatic reasons for favouring constitutional reform, particularly in terms of electoral reform and changing to a form of proportional representation. Put simply, they are the party that is most under-represented by our current First Past the Post system and, as such, they are the party set to benefit most from any reform.

Good use of "however" and "on the other hand" and "while classical liberals argue x, social liberals argue y" is the key to getting good A02 marks.

The Thirty Mark Question

This should be the question that drew you to this topic in the first place. Always make your question choices based on the essay question, as this is where the real marks can be picked up.

A few general points first:

- You *must* plan your essay
- This is your only chance to show the examiners how much you know about liberalism. Don't keep knowledge secret! Show off!

- You can always go beyond saying something "is liberal" or not: is it classically liberal? Socially liberal? Use this to add depth and evaluation to your essays.

- Maintain your focus on the question and guide the marker through your logic. Your thought process might not always be clear to the marker: relating each substantive point and/or each paragraph to the specific terms of the question would certainly help here

- Make use of as many examples as possible – current or historical (with a preference for current)

- Make sure you have read the question carefully. You might be asked to talk about "contemporary liberalism" (for example) in which case you should not waste too much time on Rousseau and Mill! Answer the question that is there, not the one you wish was there!

THIRTY MARK QUESTION (1)

Topic 1: Liberalism

02 "We are all liberals now." Discuss (30 marks)

Using material from this chapter and the hints above, attempt this question. After you've done your best, look at the back of the book to see a plan of a model answer. Make a careful note of any points that you did not include. Also make sure you make note of relevant points you made that are *not* on the model answer plan.

Liberalism glossary

Capitalism

Capitalism is an economic system based on the accumulation of capital by private individuals, called capitalists. It is usually associated with market economics as described by Adam Smith. It was famously analysed and criticised by Karl Marx in *Capital*. The ideas of liberalism emerged from capitalism and the bourgeois capitalist class.

Citizenship

Citizenship is a less straight-forward concept than it might first appear. Essentially it refers to membership of a particular nation-state. Citizenship of a country means that you have entered into a social contract: certain duties are expected of you, and certain rights are afforded to you. However, only a minority of us actually *choose* citizenship, most are born into it. There are also debates about the extent to which citizenship assumes participation and engagement in society (active citizenship).

Civil Rights

Civil rights are rights that we acquire through citizenship: they are half of a social contract. As a citizen of the United Kingdom I have the right to vote in UK General Elections. This is not a *human* or *natural* right (I can't go and vote in somebody else's election). We most associate the concept of civil rights with *campaigns* for civil rights when certain groups in a society are denied them (e.g. African Americans in some US states were denied their civil rights – as well as some basic human rights – leading to the civil rights protests of the 1960s).

Democracy

Democracy literally means "rule by the people" and is quite a disputed term! For some (including liberal philosopher, Rousseau) democracy should be *direct*. "The people" (citizens) should make the decisions themselves. In a modern liberal democratic state this is seen to be impossible (though some argue for greater use of referendums). Instead *representative democracy* is preferred, which is a form of indirect democracy. John Stuart Mill wrote at length about how representative democracy should work. In this system, we vote for representatives to make decisions on our behalf. We also have the power to remove them after a reasonable passage of time if we do not like the decisions they have taken.

Divine Right

Prior to the Enlightenment and to the development of liberal ideas, the dominant ideology in Europe was one which believed that monarchs had a *divine right* to rule: in other words, their power was granted by God and should therefore not be questioned. Of course, the power of monarchs across Europe was constantly questioned! Because God's will was expressed through the hereditary process, power struggles had to be carried out through the conduit of "rightful heirs".

The Englightenment

Also known as the "Age of Reason", the Enlightenment was a period of considerable scientific and philosophical development where reason, rationalism and science significantly undermined the supernatural assumptions at the heart of medieval society.

Equality

Equality is one of the most difficult and disputed terms in the study of political ideology. Liberals, for the most part, are interested in *equality of opportunity*. By this, we mean a level playing field. Inherited privilege, title and status should not give some a head start and hold others back. With *equality of opportunity* there will still be winners and losers, but the winners win thanks to *meritocracy* not privilege, and the losers lost in a fair fight. Some social liberals (and many socialists) prefer the concept of *equality of outcome* where you attempt to create an egalitarian society where there are mushc smaller divisions of wealth. This concept of equality might include the redistribution of wealth from the rich to the less well off.

Freedom

Freedom – or liberty – is a concept at the very heart of liberalism. We understand it in its general sense, but what does freedom really mean in the context of political ideology? "Man is born free", writes Rousseau, "but is everywhere in chains". For most liberals it is the state which imprisons people. It denies them rights, it coerces them to perform certain duties (e.g. pay tax). The people need to be freed from the state. It is important to remember that some liberals, who believed very deeply in this concept of freedom, did not believe slaves should be set free. They appeared far more concerned with the freedom of the slave owners and traders and the freedom of their market.

Hegemony

Hegemony is a word that has partly changed its meaning over time. It used to be primarily used in terms of international relations and would mean the dominant position of a particular country in a region (e.g. people might talk about US hegemony in the Middle East). The Marxist writer, Antonio Gramsci, used the term hegemony to mean the dominant position of a particular set of *ideas* in society. Liberalism is often described as the "dominant ideology" (to use the traditional Marxist tem) in modern Western society. Essay questions might well enquire the extent to which all the main parties are now dominated by liberal ideas. Another way of putting this is to say that liberalism has *hegemony* in the West: it is almost seen not as an ideology at all, but as common sense.

Human Nature

All the ideologies we consider in this book make certain assumptions about human nature. Liberalism is no different. Liberalism rather depends on the notion that individuals will act rationally.

Human Rights

Human rights are those that everybody should have, regardless of their citizenship. See *Natural Rights*.

Individualism

Liberalism *is* an individualist ideology. It is all about the freedom and rights of the individual, not about groups of people or social classes. The impact of this individualism is most apparent in economic liberalism. While the case for democratic rights, etc. benefits everybody, *economic* freedom is arguably different. The freedom of an employer to set the pay and working conditions of his/her employees can clearly come into conflict with the rights of those employees. Economic liberals see the market as the best way of resolving such conflicts (Adam Smith's

"invisible hand"), while critics would see the market as always benefiting the wealthy and powerful.

Justice

Liberals, like conservatives, believe in the rule of law. But the important part of that, for liberals, is *justice*: and that inevitably includes concepts of *equality* (everybody being treated the same before the law) and *fairness*.

Laissez-faire

Laissez-faire literally means "leave to do" or "leave it alone", but is used to refer to a free market approach to economic policy. Classical liberal economic policy sees a minimal role for the state when it comes to the economy. Through the 20th century, *laissez-faire* economics became more associated with conservatism while the development of "new liberalism" or "positive liberalism" meant that many 20th century liberals saw a greater role for the state in economic policy.

Libertarianism

Libertarianism sees a very minimal role for the state. You can have libertarianism of the left or right, although it tends to be used now to refer to right-wing libertarianism. Right-wing libertarianism then is radical, uncompromising economic liberalism: the state should keep out of economics altogether and leave the market to do its work. The term "anarcho-capitalism" is used to describe the extreme end of this viewpoint that sees the market replacing the state in pretty much all aspects of its work, including the criminal justice system, etc. Left libertarianism, on the other hand, sees collectivist solutions to state power, rather than market solutions (e.g. cooperatives, communes, etc.)

Liberty

Liberty means freedom. Often represented as a woman (as in the Statue of Liberty) Liberty was seen as a great prize to the liberals and radicals of the French Revolution and liberals across Europe and the Western world.

Natural Rights

While *civil rights* are those we enjoy as citizens, *natural rights* (or *human rights*) are those that everybody should be entitled to as a human being (e.g. the right to life).

Pluralism

Liberals favour a *pluralist* society where a number of groups and interests are able to compete for influence and power. For some this produces almost a free market of ideas, where interests compete against each other fairly and rational choices are made. The main criticisms of pluralism are *elitist* theories.

Private Property

The right to private property is central to classical liberalism. Industrialists making huge sums of money out of the capitalist system were concerned that the state could help itself to their property. This is an area where classical liberalism greatly differs from an alternative small state theory, anarchism, which argues that all private property is theft of public property.

Rights

The concept of rights is absolutely central to liberalism, but it is not an absolutely straightforward concept. Some rights are considered to be *natural* or *human rights* that we all enjoy, and others are rights that we gain as citizens (*civil rights*)

Social Contract

A Social Contract – as detailed in the book of the same name, by Jean-Jacques Rousseau – is an arrangement between the citizen and the state wherein the citizen owes certain *duties* to the state, and the state affords the citizen civil rights in exchange.

Tolerance

Liberals, especially social liberals, would assert their *tolerance*. If you, like John Stuart Mill, believe that people should be allowed to do whatever they like providing it does not affect the freedom of others, that might well involve tolerating various things of which the liberal might disapprove! However, sometimes people criticise the use of the term "tolerance" when discussing equality and diversity issues, as people would prefer to be properly accepted, rather than *tolerated*.

Utilitarianism

Utilitarianism is the term used to describe the ideas of Jeremy Bentham who was concerned about "the greatest happiness for the greatest number of people". In other words, the right decisions are those that benefit the majority. On the one hand, this appears like a basic democratic principle. However, this principle led Bentham to support the minimum possible poor relief as the rate payers in a district would be "unhappy" at having to pay for the relief of an impoverished minority.

Welfare

Welfare is a disputed issue in liberalism as social liberals see the importance of the state (or other agencies) stepping in to help the least well off in society. Classical liberals were much more likely to see welfare as an infringement of the rights of the majority in society.

SOCIALISM

A. Historical context

Some socialists suggest that the history of their ideology stretches back very far indeed. The British Labour pioneer, Keir Hardie, famously wrote about "Jesus the communist". Others point to words associated with the Peasant's Revolt ("when Adam delved and Eve span, who was then the gentleman?") Socialists like Tony Benn have written about the "socialism" of groups like the Levellers and the Diggers, who talked about the Earth being "a common treasury" for everybody to share during the 17th century English Revolution. More recently, there were socialists on the fringes of radical movements like the Chartists. There is certainly a long, radical tradition in the UK which both socialists and liberals can claim as their own.

The socialism that was to come to be such a significant world ideology from the late 19th century onwards can be seen, in part at least, as a response to liberalism. Socialists found liberalism an unsatisfactory answer to an ill-divided world. Socialists felt that society was unequal and unjust and that freeing individuals from the state did not come close to dealing with the real problems. Society had to be changed entirely; the world had to be "turned upside down". Although the issue of *class* was not equally central to all forms of socialism, at the heart of socialism is a concept of freeing the working class as a whole from oppression, not just the individual. Socialism is essentially and definitively a *collectivist* ideology.

In 1848, Karl Marx and Friedrich Engels wrote *The Communist Manifesto*. This famous work outlined one particular form of socialism (Communism, or Marxism) and, along with Marx's more analytical and academic work, had a profound influence on international politics. At the time it was written, however, "the spectre haunting Europe" that Marx and Engels wrote of was really a very small spectre.

There were socialist parties and movements around Europe, mostly of the *Utopian* sort of which Marx did not really approve, but they had rarely had much influence. Very few people were "communist". Through the rest of the century, however, socialism (in all its forms) was the world's fastest growing political ideology.

Dictionary definitions often reduce socialism to a purely economic idea, where public ownership of industry is preferred to the private ownership apparent under capitalism. This does not come close to explaining the ideology of most socialists, which is a much broader critique of capitalist society and how to make society better, considering many more aspects of society than just who owns industry.

By the late 19th century, there were several broadly socialist groups in Britain. These included:

The ILP. The Independent Labour Party was formed in Bradford in the 1880s with the specific aim of getting working-class people into parliament. With considerable overlaps with non-conformist religion and the radical wing of the Liberals, the ILP's socialism was strongly rooted in ethics, morality and a belief that capitalism was an evil. The membership of the ILP was largely working class.

The SDF. The Social Democratic Federation was Britain's Marxist party. They believed their socialism to be of a decidedly *scientific* kind, as opposed to the "utopian" and *ethical* nature of many of their contemporaries. They believed that their analysis of capitalism, and their proposal of socialism, was based on scientific and objective study, rather than on emotion or religious conviction. Some more "emotional" members broke away to form other groups (such as the great artist and writer, William Morris, who formed the Socialist League, described as "anarcho-communist").

The Clarion Movement. Built around the *Clarion* newspaper, Robert Blatchford's group saw socialism as much more than a political ideology, preferring to see it as a whole way of life. Through the newspaper, Blatchford's books, like *Merrie England* and *Britain for the British*, and the work of cultural organizations like choirs and cycling clubs, the Clarion movement is credited with having made very many "converts".

The Fabian Society. The Fabian Society, like the SDF, were proud of taking an objective, scientific and analytical approach to socialism. A mixture of socialists and radical liberals, they believed that capitalism could not be replaced in a rush of revolution, but rather a *gradualist* approach should be taken. Fabians were predominantly middle class and included well-known writers and intellectuals (e.g. H.G. Wells and Edith Nesbit)

Despite many changes, not least the creation of new organisations like the Labour and Communist parties, these different approaches and analyses are apparent throughout the history of British socialism.

At the same time as the growth and development of these socialist organisations, there were large changes afoot in the trade union movement. Small trade guilds were merging to form large general unions, like the Transport and General Workers' Union, representing large numbers of workers. The Trade Unions saw the need for political representation and sponsored some Liberal MPs (known as Lib-Labs). For Britain's nascent socialist movement to gain leadership of the organised working class and form a real labour movement, it needed to convince the trade union movement.

In 1900, a new group set about doing just that. The Labour Representation Committee (LRC) was established with the specific aim of getting working-class people properly represented in parliament, and it brought together many of the aforementioned socialist organisations with the general unions.

Britain's two-party system, of Tories and Liberals, was under significant threat from the left. Socialist politics were to be catapulted from the fringe to centre-stage.

In 1906 the Labour Representation Committee changed its name to the Labour Party. Within eighteen years it was forming its first government. This rapid growth was not without incident, and many of the tensions that have continued to exist within labour politics were already apparent.

Disappointed at a lack of Marxist analysis at the heart of Labour, the SDF left the Party and formed the British Socialist Party. Years later, following the Russian Revolution of 1917, the BSP transformed itself into the Communist Party.

There were large and acrimonious divisions over the subject of the First World War. Many leading Labour figures (especially those associated with the largely pacifist ILP) strongly opposed Britain's role in the War, while others saw such a position as unpatriotic.

Arguments over just how socialist the Labour Party ought to be, and about its views on major international controversies and conflicts, have continued to plague the Labour Party for the rest of its history.

Despite all of this, the Labour Party maintained its *federal* structure, where affiliated organisations and trade unions had a clear role in the party while remaining independent in their own right.

In 1918, the Labour Party developed a new constitution, written by the Fabians, Sydney and Beatrice Webb. Clause IV, part four, of the new constitution was to be at the heart of two battles for the Labour Party's soul, in the 1950s and the 1990s.

CLAUSE IV PART FOUR OF THE OLD LABOUR PARTY CONSTITUTION (1918-1995):

To secure for the workers, by hand or by brain, the full fruits of their industry and the most equitable distribution thereof that may be possible based upon the common ownership of the means of production, distribution and exchange, and the best obtainable system of popular administration and control of each industry or service.

The reference here to the *common ownership of the means of production, distribution and exchange* has tended to be taken to mean *nationalisation* or state ownership, although there are other forms of common ownership popular amongst socialists (such as cooperatives).

Whatever the radical aspirations of the Labour Party in its constitutional "aims and objectives", the first two Labour governments were both minority governments and achieved rather little. Socialists may have thronged the streets of London singing "The Red Flag" on the election of Labour's first Prime Minister, but the fears of much of the British establishment were put to rest. Ramsay MacDonald was no longer a radical, and his government did not challenge either capitalism or Britain's class structure.

The fears were perhaps understandable. As the British franchise grew, with more and more working-class people getting the vote, there was a genuine fear that socialism – as an ideology that promised radical improvements for that class – might find a permanent majority and that "the tyranny of the majority" might take revenge upon the privileged minority.

An early clue that Ramsay MacDonald would not rock the boat was his decision not to include the radical socialist George Lansbury in his first cabinet, despite his great popularity in the Labour Party. Lansbury had been to the newly-formed Soviet Russia and had shaken Lenin by the hand; King George V was not prepared to shake hands with a new minister who had shaken hands with "his cousin's murderer".

Even so, the secret services conspired against that first minority Labour government, leaking a fake Russian letter ("the Zinoviev letter") that stirred up "Reds under the beds" fears. This was the start of a difficult relationship between Labour and the security services.

Other points of note before Labour got its first majority government are:

The General Strike – Some socialists thought it was the revolution; eventually the Labour and TUC leadership were seen by revolutionaries as having betrayed their members and the working class.

Ramsay MacDonald's Defection – Labour's second minority government ended with their leader and Prime Minister leaving the party and remaining Prime Minister of a national coalition government. The Labour Party became a small rump under George Lansbury's leadership.

The Second World War was to have a massive impact on socialism in the UK. Despite two Labour governments, socialist policies had still not been seen in Britain, and many people were frightened of them.

But Winston Churchill's wartime coalition government included a number of Labour ministers in key departments, and involved a considerable amount of central economic planning and even some nationalisation. Not only was this not the end of the world, many saw this planning of an economy as remarkably sensible, especially in the context of the Great Depression that had preceded the war, which was seen by many as the failure of a laissez-faire approach to the economy.

The experience of the Great Depression was to have a further impact. The liberal, Lloyd George, had promised "homes fit for heroes" following the First World War, but people's experiences, particularly in the more industrial parts of the UK, were anything but that. Long-term unemployment and absolute poverty had fed the demand for radical change.

Socialist ideas about welfare had also been given a boost by a high-profile and respected report by the liberal, William Beveridge, that recommended the creation of a Welfare State.

All of these factors together led to Labour's landslide victory in 1945

The 1945-51 Attlee Government

Clement Attlee was no great radical, but his government did include some radical ministers and in six years it did a lot to transform Britain. The Marxist Health and Housing minister, Aneurin Bevan, from a working-class Welsh mining background, was at the forefront of reform. He undertook a massive council house building programme and, perhaps most significant of all, created the National Health Service. The government also nationalised a number of key industries, including coal and steel, and carefully managed and planned the economy to prevent a slump, even maintaining wartime rations.

As early as 1947, a group of Labour MPs formed the Keep Left group, warning that the party was abandoning its socialist roots. In 1950, resigning ministers including Nye Bevan and future Prime Minister, Harold Wilson, swelled the ranks of this Keep Left group and it turned into the Bevanites.

Clement Attlee

Through the 1950s, the great debate between traditional democratic socialists and *revisionists* was played out between the Bevanites and the Gaitskellites. The Gaitskellites were in charge (Hugh Gaitskell replaced Attlee as the leader of the Labour Party in opposition). The Gaitskellites attempted a kind of New Labour transformation of the party (Gaitskell tried and failed to remove Clause IV, later removed by Tony Blair). The Bevanites (who dominated local Labour parties and were popular in some of the trade unions) defended the party's socialist and internationalist beliefs and also fought hard against nuclear weapons.

Gaitskell made two famous, significant conference speeches. In one he remarked that local Labour parties were riddled with "Communists" (quite an extraordinary attack on his own party). In another, after losing a vote on nuclear disarmament to the Bevanite majority, he vowed to "fight, fight and fight again to save the party I love."

However, even Bevan had quite a *pragmatic* approach to his socialism. He upset many of his followers by eventually preferring *multilateral disarmament* to *unilateral disarmament* in a famous conference speech where he said that a unilateral policy would mean a Labour Foreign Secretary would be left "naked" when meeting other nations.

KEY QUOTATION:

"The religion of socialism is the language of priorities."
- Aneurin Bevan

The Bevanites could be said to have won the battle: Gaitskell's successor as leader of the Labour Party was Bevanite, Harold Wilson. However, while Bevanites and other left-wing figures did well under Wilson (like Michael Foot and Tony Benn), Gaitskellites like Denis Healey did even better. While Wilson tried to keep the party united, for the most part it was the right-wing of the party that maintained the ascendency.

The Road to New Labour

During the 1970s, there was a growth of support, once again, for the *left wing* of the Labour Party among its members. Furthermore, the old Bevanites in the Tribune Group began to be seen as quite moderate parts of the establishment, and a new left grew up, and their hero in parliament was Tony Benn. Benn contested the Deputy Leadership of the Party in 1981 but was beaten by a very narrow margin by Denis Healey in a bitter contest between left and right. The SDP (who were on the right of the Labour Party) broke away shortly afterwards, leading many to assume that Benn's faction would become dominant. However, former Bennite Neil Kinnock replaced Michael Foot as party leader and began a long period of "modernisation" that would ultimately lead to "New Labour". By the 1997 General Election, the "old" Labour Left, still eloquently led by Tony Benn, had become a small rump in a party now dominated by a different Tony B.

New Labour

Some argue that Tony Blair was the deciding factor in Labour's 1997 landslide result. Others suggest that his predecessor, John Smith, would also have been successful in that election had he lived. Whichever version is true, there is no escaping the fact that New Labour was a formidable election-winning machine, achieving landslides in 1997 and 2001 and even winning in 2005. By 2005 Blair was unpopular and New Labour, that had once been associated with Britpop and "Cool Britannia", had been tarnished by the Iraq War. When Blair was replaced by Gordon Brown he had certainly changed the Labour Party in quite fundamental ways. However, essentially it was still the same party that emerged from the First World War, with its federal structure and tight link to the trade union movement. Although Blair had replaced the controversial Clause IV of the party's constitution, it remained a party attached to the trade union movement and formally committed to a form of socialism.

After New Labour

On his election as party leader, Ed Miliband declared that New Labour "was dead". However, this did not indicate a swing "back" to "Old Labour" and the ideological direction of the party is still very much "up for grabs", with social democracy being campaigned for by Compass, democratic socialism being campaigned for by the Labour Representation Committee, a continued commitment to New Labour being pushed for by Progress and other groups suggesting new approaches again (such as "Blue Labour").

B. Varieties of socialism

Socialism can be divided up into a number of key varieties, all with a clear tradition in the history detailed in the previous section.

Democratic Socialism This is a broad term to describe the ideology that wishes to replace capitalism with socialism and believes that this can be done through democratic means. The whole Labour Party variety of socialism *might* be described as "democratic socialist", and indeed the "new" Clause IV from 1995 begins "we are a democratic socialist party". However, some modern Labour traditions might be questioned as to whether they are socialist at all.

> KEY QUOTATION:
>
> "The Labour Party has never been a socialist party, but it has always had socialists in it"
> - Tony Benn

As such, "democratic socialist" is more usually used to describe the position of the Labour Left, what came to be called "Old Labour" in the 1990s. Tony Benn could be seen as a key proponent or, in the current Parliamentary Labour Party, John

McDonnell or Jeremy Corbyn. Democratic socialists from history would include Aneurin (Nye) Bevan.

Other terms that might be used:

- Labour Left

- Hard Left

- "Old Labour"

Related organisations:

- The Labour Party

- The Socialist Campaign Group

- The Labour Representation Committee

- The Tribune Group

Revolutionary Socialism While democratic socialists believe society can be transformed through the ballot box, revolutionaries believe democratic means will not work. They would argue that the establishment, with all the means at its disposal, will prevent any genuine attempt to turn Britain socialist. Revolutionary socialism has always been a minority position in the UK and has been divided between Trotskyites and Communists since the Stalin era in the Soviet Union. While members of the official Communist Party remained supportive of Soviet Russia, the Trotskyites became its fiercest set of critics. There has always been a revolutionary element on the fringes of the Labour Party. Both Hugh Gaitskell and Neil Kinnock, as party leaders, confronted Labour's revolutionaries. Gaitskell, in the 1950s, complained of local Labour parties being full of Communists, while Kinnock confronted the Militant Tendency, a Trotskyite group that had come to dominate Labour's youth wing and some local councils.

Other terms that might be used:

- Marxists

- Trotskyites ("Trots")

- Communists ("Tankies")

Related organisations:

- Socialist Workers Party

- The Communist Party of Britain

Utopian Socialism The idea of Utopia is one of an imagined perfect future state. Many socialists, on criticising capitalism and proposing their socialist alternative, have been asked to give details about what a socialist future might look like. Such descriptions are "Utopian" and socialists whose ideas are largely based on such descriptions are called Utopian Socialists. William Morris, the famous artist and writer, was a famous Utopian. His book *News From Nowhere* is a good example of the Utopian imagination. Many of the socialists associated with the Clarion movement of the late 19th century were also Utopians, such as the poet Edward Carpenter. While some socialists are very critical of Utopianism, considering it idealistic and lacking in serious analysis, it would certainly appear that Utopianism captured more people's imagination than more "scientific" Marxist tracts of the same period.

Other terms that might be used:

- Religion of Socialism

- Guild Socialism

- Ethical Socialism

Related organisations:

- The ILP

- The Socialist League

- Clarion

Social Democracy Social Democracy is a term that has completely changed its meaning over the last 100 years or so. Britain's Social Democratic Federation and Russia's Social Democrats were both Marxist organisations. In the late 19th century and early 20th century, for a party to be called Social Democratic rather than Labour (for example) would suggest that they were more avowedly socialist, and probably Marxist. Social Democracy, in this context, was seen as a route to socialism, and as such could be almost interchangeable with "democratic socialism".

But at some point, social democracy came to be an end in itself, rather than a route to socialism, and this became the normal, mainstream position of most European Labour, Social Democratic or Socialist parties. This version of social democracy wishes to make modern capitalism better; it has no aspiration to replace it. This would lead some to conclude that modern social democracy was not socialist at all.

KEY QUOTATION:

"Socialism is whatever the Labour Party happens to be doing at the time."
 - Herbert Morrison

While New Labour might be a good example of modern social democracy in action, others would argue that New Labour was more right-wing than social democracy.

Certainly the social democrats who left Labour in the early 1980s to form the SDP (and eventually the Liberal Democrats) found some of New Labour's agenda uncomfortable and to the right of where they considered themselves to be.

Other terms that might be used:

- Fabianism
- Revisionism
- Gradualism
- New Labour

Associated organisations:

- The Labour Party
- Party of European Socialists
- Fabian Society
- Progress

"Old Labour"	"New Labour"
Predominantly working class	Predominantly middle class
Equality of outcome	Equality of opportunity
Common ownership	Preference for private ownership
Trade Unions	Business
Unilateral nuclear disarmament	Pro-nuclear
"Non-aligned" foreign policy	Pro-American
Often radical on constitutional reform but less of a priority than social reform	Focus on constitutional reform

C. Socialism and contemporary party politics

Only one of the UK's main political parties considers itself to be a socialist party: the Labour Party. But just how socialist *is* the modern Labour Party? And are there elements of socialism among the policies of the other parties?

The Labour Party

"The Labour Party is a democratic socialist party", according to the cards held by its members. However, the quotation comes from Tony Blair's Clause IV of the Party's constitution which goes on to commit the party to the "rigours of competition" and the "dynamism of the market", neo-liberal aspirations that even revisionist socialists of the past would not have recognised as their own. It is clear that Labour in government sought to be a "pro-business" party. Blair declared that trade unions could expect "fairness not favours" from a Labour government. While this might seem a perfectly reasonable idea, the trade union movement clearly sees itself as an essential part of the labour movement, not just as "any other pressure group". New Labour, in government, made no attempts to reverse the "anti-trade union" laws brought in during the Thatcher government. Nor did they attempt to reverse any Conservative privatisations, even hugely unpopular ones like the privatisation of the railways.

For the vast majority of its time in government, New Labour could be seen – in economic terms – as anything but socialist. However, others would point to the minimum wage. A minimum wage had been a Labour aspiration since the earliest days of the party, but no previous Labour government had managed to implement it. Revisionists would further argue that socialism today – their form of socialism – was not "anti-business" and did not depend upon nationalisation or muscular trade unionism.

For them, socialism is about fairness, equality of opportunity and social justice.

The Conservative Party

Is there any evidence of socialism in the modern Conservative Party? You wouldn't really expect to see it. In some ways modern conservatism (since the 1970s) has partly been defined against socialist ideas: it is about small government, laissez-faire economics, etc. However, it has been argued that David Cameron was influenced by New Labour, and some have described Cameron as the "heir to Blair".

While this should be seen in the context of New Labour having been greatly influenced by the New Right government of Margaret Thatcher, can we see any ideological evidence of these Labour influences on Cameron?

In terms of *rhetoric*, in the lead up to the 2010 General Election, David Cameron made many references to his support for the National Health Service. However, his government then went on to attempt a major reorganisation of the NHS that was more radically New Right than anything Margaret Thatcher ever attempted. This is one of many examples of the New Labour influence on modern Conservatism being more of rhetoric, branding and marketing than of ideology.

There are examples of the modern Conservative Party taking an interest in social exclusion and fairness, that might indicate a social democrat influence, however the proposed solutions to problems are always small state or "Big Society" solutions and the concerns could be more indicative of a one nation or paternalistic concern rather than a social democrat or socialist one.

ACTIVITY: CONSERVATIVE PARTY POLICY TODAY

As previously with other parties, go to the Conservatives' website (http://www.conservatives.com) and find a section on there detailing their newest most up-to-date policies. Here, again, on no more than one side of A4 for each policy, analyse a number of these in terms of how *socialist* they are. File these carefully with the rest!

The Liberal Democrat Party

The Liberal Democrat Party was formed from the merging of the old Liberal Party with the Social Democrat Party which had split from the Labour Party. As the SDP broke from the Labour Party *partly* because of the socialist "Bennite" ascendency in the late 1970s and early 1980s (as well as over policies on the European Union and on nuclear disarmament) you might not expect to see much *socialism* in the Liberal Democrat Party, but might expect to evidence of *social democracy*.

Interestingly, as the Labour Party moved to the *right* under the leadership of Tony Blair, some began to see the Liberal Democrats as Britain's most left-wing party. During this period, they tended to oppose the introduction of private finance and market mechanisms into public services, campaigned for free university education, argued in favour of tax rises for specific spending commitments and were the only mainstream party to oppose the Iraq War. In these positions they found themselves in regular agreement with the *left-wing* MPs in the Labour Party who were regular rebels on these kinds of issues. Interestingly, the left-wing Labour MPs also tended to rebel on a number of key *liberal* issues relating to anti-terror legislation, again finding themselves voting alongside Liberal Democrats.

Clearly here the *social democrat* element in the Liberal Democrat Party, in alliance with the *social liberals* found more common cause with the democratic socialists in the Labour Party than with the leading New Labour element. However, in more recent times, the Orange Book liberals in the Liberal Democrat Party have made a conscious effort to move the party away from the left and back towards the centre and even the centre right. Their economic liberalism is at odds with the social democratic core of the Liberal Democrat party, but paradoxically brought the Liberal Democrats closer to the ideological position of New Labour.

However, in coalition with the Conservative Party, very few elements of social democracy appear to have survived. The Liberal Democrats *did* successfully push for a raise in the tax-free allowance bringing a number of low-paid people out paying tax and also led the internal opposition to the coalition government's reform package for the NHS. However, it could be argued that the latter campaign was more as a result of the Liberal Democrat's dreadful showing in local elections in 2011 than because of traces of social democratic ideology.

ACTIVITY: LIBERAL DEMOCRAT PARTY POLICY TODAY

Go onto the Liberal Democrat Party's website (http://www.libdems.org.uk) and find a handful of their current, bang up-to-date policies. On no more than one sheet of A4 for each policy, analyse them in terms of their *socialism*.
Remember to consider whether *all* socialists would approve or disapprove of the policy in question and why.

D. Answering exam questions on socialism

Refer back to Liberalism for general instructions on answering 10 mark and 30 mark questions.

Topic 2

01 What is the difference between social democracy and democratic socialism? (10 marks)

This is a *compare and contrast* question again, so we need to clearly define the two terms and pick out some key differences and controversies to get our ten marks.

Clearly for some in the modern Labour Party there is little or no difference between social democracy and democratic socialism. The Labour Party's constitution includes the phrase "we are a democratic socialist party" and yet, certainly since the arrival of New Labour, they might be more accurately described as "social democratic".

The traditional understanding of "democratic socialist" is one in which capitalism will be replaced by socialism, but that this shall be done through democratic means. This was the political position of many in the early Labour Party and might be the best description of the political views of those on the *left* of the Labour Party today, e.g. Tony Benn.

Social democracy, on the other hand, has come to mean a reformist type of politics that seeks to make possible reforms to capitalism in order to ensure that its social impact is minimised. As such, there is clearly a great deal of overlap between democratic socialism and social democracy, but socialists and social democrats have a different *end point* in sight.

In Britain, it might well be the case that social democrats see less of a key role for trade unions and have less of a clear dimension of *social class* in their politics than democratic socialists do. While some might suggest that Old Labour is democratic socialist and New Labour social democrat, others would point out that New Labour is some way to the right of what we might traditionally mean by social democracy, and that many Old Labour people on the party's left wing fit the description "social democrat" quite neatly.

A different sort of ten mark question might be:

01   Why do socialists traditionally favour nationalisation / public ownership?   (10 marks)

Again, we need to define the terms (nationalisation and public ownership) but we are also asked to contextualise this and are posed quite a difficult question: *why* do socialists favour it? An answer to this question might look something like:

Although the modern Labour Party favours a mixed economy, with perhaps a preference for private ownership, socialists have traditionally wanted to see public ownership and past Labour governments (such as the 1945-51 Attlee government) have *nationalised* certain industries, and Labour oppositions opposed the *privatisations* of the Thatcher and Major governments.

Although there are a variety of forms of common ownership (e.g. cooperatives), public ownership is generally used to describe the ownership of an industry or service by the state. Socialists favour this because they are critical of *capitalism* and the powerful position of the capitalists compared with the workers. They see state ownership of industry as being *democratic* ownership, and therefore the workers have considerably more control over their lives than under private ownership. Socialists are also sceptical about the benefits of a free market and, as such, favour *economic planning*. Labour governments felt that some industries, especially public utilities, could be better planned if they were publically owned (hence the nationalisation of the railways, coal, steel, etc.)

From the 1950s, a number of socialists ("revisionists") preferred to focus on outcomes and concluded that *ownership* was not especially important, provided there were equal or socially just outcomes. Traditional socialists continued to argue that ownership went hand-in-hand with power and control, and therefore public ownership was an integral part of democratic socialism.

Thirty-mark Question (2)

Read the following thirty mark question. Using the book, the website, your notes and the general guidance for thirty-mark questions contained in the Liberalism section, attempt it. Then look at the model answer plan at the back of the book.

Topic 2	Socialism
02	"The Labour Party is a democratic socialist party." Discuss (30 marks)

E. Socialism Glossary

Class Conflict

The concept of class conflict is particularly relevant to Marxism. Marx wrote that "the history of all hitherto existing society is the history of class struggle". Capitalist society was based on the struggle between the bourgeoisie (the ruling class) and the proletariat (the working class). Socialists are on the side of the working class.

Class Consciousness

Another important concept for Marxists, the extent to which people are *conscious* of their class is decidedly important. It is only when people are conscious of their class and the exploitation of their class, that they will develop revolutionary ideas. Marx felt that many workers had a "false consciousness" where they were encouraged to feel that things were not so bad, or that they were lucky, or that their interests coincided with those of their employers.

Collectivism

Socialism is a *collectivist* ideology. Even in the Labour Party's "new" 1995 constitution there is the statement: "we believe that by the strength of our common endeavour we achieve more than we do alone". Socialist ideas are based on cooperation, common endeavour and working together. One of the key ways that socialism can be distinguished from radical forms of liberalism is the primacy of the individual in liberal thought.

Common Ownership

Common ownership is actually quite a general term. The use of the term in the Labour Party's old constitution was always taken to mean *public ownership* (i.e. industries owned by a democratic state) but many socialists would point to alternative forms of common ownership such as cooperatives and mutual societies.

Communism

At one time, the word "communism" was more-or-less synonymous with "socialism" but, since the Russian Revolution of 1917, it has come to be associated with a very specific type of politics. When governments such as the current Chinese government describe themselves as "Communist" it is hard to find much remaining of the word's socialist roots. Communist China is characterised by rampant capitalism, great inequality and an absence of democracy. Indeed it is not so different from the societies that socialism emerged to try and change.

Democracy

The link between socialism and *democracy* is a very important one. For some socialists, like Tony Benn, the two are inextricably linked and you can't have one without the other. For these *democratic socialists*, socialism is all about extending and improving democracy. Of course, some organisations and governments that have described themselves as socialist have been decidedly undemocratic.

Democratic Socialism

Democratic socialism is a type of socialist ideology that sees a parliamentary and democratic road to socialism, as distinct from revolutionary socialists.

Equality

The concept of equality is very important to socialism. Most socialists (apart from some "revisionists" and social democrats) would argue that *equality of outcome* is much more important than *equality of opportunity*. They would argue that apparent *equality of opportunity* or *meritocracy* is often little more than an ideological justification for maintaining inequality. In a deeply divided and unequal society, arguing that everybody had the same *opportunity* does not solve the problem of the poverty of those at the bottom. This is why socialists favour the redistribution of wealth through such means as progressive taxation.

Fabianism

Fabianism refers specifically to ideas put forward over the years by The Fabian Society, one of the founding "socialist societies" of the Labour Party and now a think-tank or internal pressure group in the Labour Party. Former Fabians have come from both "wings" of the party (Tony Benn and Tony Blair have both written Fabian pamphlets) but it is certainly more associated with the party's social democratic right wing. Fabianism is generally seen as Labour's *intellectual* right wing, closely related to gradualism and revisionism.

Fraternity

Trade unionists still address each other as "brothers and sisters" and this suggestion of a *familial relationship* is important to the working-class movement and socialist politics. It goes hand in hand with *solidarity*; to suggest that workers are brothers (and, once feminism began to influence socialism, sisters) further emphasises that they should be collaborative and work together for their shared, class interests, rather than take an individualist approach.

Gradualism

The most famous "gradualists" are the Fabians and it suggests an alternative to *revolutionary* socialism, sometimes called *evolutionary socialism*. Rather than changing everything over night in a revolutionary upheaval, gradualists want to make incremental changes based on priorities and what is possible. Some modern "gradualists" might be accused by more traditional socialists of having abandoned an ultimate socialist goal altogether.

Nationalisation

Nationalisation refers very specifically to the purchase (or requisition!) of companies or industries by the government. The Labour government of 1945-51 undertook a number of successful nationalisations. In 1983 Labour manifesto, Labour promised to nationalise the "commanding heights of the economy". Some socialists have criticised the model of nationalisation employed by the 45-51 government (associated with the minister Herbert Morrison and therefore described as "Morrisonian nationalisation").

Public Ownership

The Labour Party's famous original Clause IV (that lasted from 1918 to 1994) stated that the party believed in the "common ownership of the means of production, distribution and exchange": a constitutional commitment to socialism.

Revisionism

The right-wing of the Labour Party, from the 1950s, engaged in *revisionism*: revisiting socialism in the context of an apparently more affluent society. Tony Crosland was a key figure. For the revisionists social justice, fairness and equality were more important than economic changes. Essentially, the revisionists had a social democratic view rather than a socialist one.

Social Democracy

Social democracy is a term that has changed its meaning over the years. Today it relates to a left-of-centre politics that promotes social reform under capitalism. New Labour was often described as social democrat (rather than socialist) although some questioned whether New Labour was sufficiently left wing or radical to even be fairly described as social democrat.

Social Exclusion

Particularly during the New Labour era, the emphasis of the Labour Party shifted away from *the working class* to the poor and socially-excluded. The suggestion was that the vast majority of people were not essentially "middle class" but that policies were needed to help engage and include a tiny minority. This does not sit very comfortably with a traditional socialist analysis of inequality and class.

Social Justice

New Labour thinkers were also concerned with what they called "social justice". It was sometimes used as an alternative term to socialism. Essentially it was a focus on *fairness*. Social exclusion was unjust and unfair and had to be tackled.

Solidarity

Solidarity is a key principle of socialism and of trade unionism. It refers specifically to the collectivist principle of socialism: people work together as a movement and stand side by side. One example would be international solidarity where socialists in one country will support (by a variety of means) the campaigns and struggles of socialists elsewhere. Similarly members of one trade union might want to try and show solidarity with members of another union in struggle/dispute. However "solidarity" strike action (like the General Strike of 1926) is now illegal.

Utopianism

Some socialism is considered to be "Utopian". Utopia is an imagined perfect future. Some socialists, such as William Morris (in his book *News From Nowhere*) focus on what a perfect, socialist future state might look like. Karl Marx was quite dismissive of Utopian socialists.

Wealth Distribution

Socialists have traditionally been very concerned with the distribution of wealth in society. It is for that reason that many socialists see progressive taxation and public spending as a method of *redistribution* of wealth. However, some modern social democrats or New Labour figures have expressed a different view. Peter Mandelson said he was "comfortable" with people becoming "filthy rich" under a Labour government.

CONSERVATISM

A. Historical context

Conservatism has its roots in the late 18th century and was a reaction against liberalism, radicalism and the European spirit of revolution and the perceived threat that these ideas posed to British traditions.

One of the founding fathers of British conservatism was the parliamentarian and philosopher Edmumd Burke. Burke feared that a particular form of British liberty was under threat from the radical views of the French Revolution. For Burke, British people's ancient liberties were protected by *tradition*. Traditional conservatism, which is greatly associated with Burke, is based upon the following elements of British society:

Hierarchy: Traditional conservatives believe that people have their station in society and should know their place. People should respect their betters, and people should also be aware of the responsibilities that come with superiority.

Monarchy: The Monarchy provides continuity and stability to Britain's constitution. This unifying national figurehead acts as social cement, uniting the nation.

Aristocracy: Some people *are* better. It is important that the best families maintain their status in society and that property passes down through these family lines. This too acts as social cement.

The Church of England: Another great British institution is the Church. This provides people with a moral code, justifies the hierarchy and helps to apply the aforementioned cement!

Nation / Patriotism: Of huge importance to traditional conservatism is a love for the nation. Rather than have people fragmented in a variety of interests (and classes, etc.) people should be united in their love of nation, obedience to the Crown and clear sense of position and status.

The Tories then, who were the party of traditional conservatism, represented the aristocrats in the late 18th and early 19th century. They stood against the revolutionary spirit of the age, coming into conflict even in Britain in events like the Peterloo massacre in Manchester in 1819.

There were two main problems for conservatives in early 19th century Britain. First, their class (the old aristocracy) was clearly losing out, economically speaking, to the new class of industrialists (the bourgeoisie). Second, as Whig governments slowly increased the *franchise* (who was entitled to vote), the Tories found themselves representing a smaller and smaller minority of the electorate. There needed to be a significant change.

One change came from the new class of industrialists themselves. As people made huge sums of money in the industrial revolution, many of the winners aspired to the lives, lifestyles and political attitudes of the old aristocracy. Milltown millionaires moved out to grand piles in the countryside and often saw keen support for the Tory Party as an important element of that social elevation. It went both ways of course, because some of the old aristocrats saw opportunities in *capitalism* and, with that, began to embrace *some* of the key ideas of the liberal ideology that surrounded it. In particular, gentleman capitalists saw the benefits of economic liberalism. Traditional conservatives had found rapid industrialisation upsetting to the natural order of things and found free markets to be dangerous things. The paternalism of traditional conservatism – that viewed the lower orders like children – consequently viewed child labour, poor working conditions and the slave trade as evils to be opposed. But as the interests of the aristocracy and the bourgeoisie converged, the appeal of free markets and the evils of state intervention became more apparent.

Increasingly, through the 19th century, the Conservative Party came to mostly represent the rich (whether that be "old" or "new" money) whereas, when the Whigs became the Liberal Party, they came more to represent other sections of society. The Conservatives' traditional views also always managed to attract a section of the "lower orders" of society. Some working-class people saw the Conservative Party as the *patriotic* choice and this became more apparent in the late 19th and early 20th centuries when people came to closely associate the Conservative Party with Empire, greatness, the union with Ireland and feared that Liberals were associated with *foreign* ideas, supported Home Rule for Ireland and all sorts of other abhorrent positions!

Nationalism and patriotism among the working class was also bolstered by nationalistic popular culture, such as music hall songs like "By Jingo!" (the song which the word "jingoism" derives from). This *jingoistic* element of British Conservatism remained a key element of the party's appeal, helping to account for the upsurge in popularity for Margaret Thatcher during the Falklands conflict, for example.

While this is one way to explain how an increase in the franchise did not spell trouble for the Conservative Party, there was also the impact of the *One Nation* conservatism of Benjamin Disraeli. Disraeli feared that industrialism had turned Britain into two nations, the rich and the poor. He saw it as part of the duty of the Conservative Party to heal that rift. While part of this was through the traditional conservative approach of appealing to unifying traditions and institutions, another part was in promoting policies that would ameliorate the problems of the poorest. In other words, the one nation tradition in conservatism saw some role for the state in helping the poor. Disraeli's Conservative Party recognised the importance, in a new world of mass elections, of mass support and "membership". The "Primrose League" (named after Disraeli's favourite flower) was a mass membership organisation dedicated to supporting the Conservative Party and was proud to be populated by many working-class conservatives.

Therefore, through the 19th century, the Tories had managed to wear many hats: the paternalistic one, the traditional one, the laissez-faire one, the "one nation" one and the jingoistic one. Clearly there are overlaps: "one nation" conservatism embodies many of the more positive elements of traditional conservatism: paternalistic and unifying. However, this "shape-shifting" has led many to question whether conservatism should be described as an ideology at all. Conservatives themselves are at the forefront of this argument: many Conservatives have argued that conservatism is essentially *pragmatic* and not ideological at all.

There are times in the 20th century history of the Conservative Party where that pragmatism is entirely apparent (such as the long period of post-war consensus in the 1940s, 50s and 60s where the Conservative leadership accepted that a welfare state and a mixed economy essentially *worked* and should therefore be maintained). David Cameron appealed to a similar "anti-ideology" sentiment when talking about his party's commitment to the NHS. However, at other times, the 20th century Conservative Party appeared deeply ideological, such as in the years leading up to the First World War when the party's traditional opposition to Home Rule for

Ireland became deeply radical, and – most famously – in the 1980s when the government was led by Margaret Thatcher, described by Peter Pugh and Carl Flint as "the most nakedly ideological British politician in the latter half of the 20th century.") Another deeply ideological 20th century politician, the socialist Tony Benn, described Margaret Thatcher as "a great ideologue".

The committed ideologues of the New Right set about dismantling the post-war consensus (that appeared to have stopped working, judging from the economic crises of the 1970s) and set about attacking trade unionism and socialism with extraordinary vigour. When Margaret Thatcher said her greatest achievement was New Labour, she meant it. For her, it was the destruction of socialism as a force in modern Britain.

The key debate that took place within the Conservative Party in the decade immediately following the Thatcher years, particularly under the leaderships of Major and Hague, was the Europe debate. Although Margaret Thatcher had signed the Single European Act, by the end of her premiership she had developed a much more sceptical attitude to the European project. Her devotees on the right wing of the Conservative Party increasingly became fully and unequivocally *eurosceptic*. While some key Conservatives, like Michael Heseltine and Kenneth Clarke, remained committed *europhiles*, they became increasingly isolated in the party.

While John Major managed to get the Maastricht Treaty through parliament, despite the efforts of the "bastards"[1] in his cabinet, the 2001 Conservative General Election campaign was fought on entirely eurosceptic lines. A vote for the Conservative Party would, it was claimed, "save the pound". Strangely, although many opinion polls indicated that the British public tended towards euroscepticism, the Conservative Party's apparent pre-occupation with Europe proved unpopular in the polls. This might partly have been because the eurosceptic vote was regularly split by single-issue parties (like the UK Independence Party) as well as there being some eurosceptics who otherwise supported the Labour Party. As such, the issue of Europe became a "toxic" one for the Conservative Party and, under Michael Howard and more especially under David Cameron, the topic became almost taboo.

A combination of memories of Margaret Thatcher's approach to welfare, the preoccupation with Europe and another apparent preoccupation with immigration and asylum, led to the Conservative Party being thought of by many as "the nasty party". It was part of David Cameron's agenda to reverse this; to rescue the Conservative Party's brand.

---

[1] John Major spoke of his eurosceptic cabinet colleagues as "bastards" when he thought the cameras had stopped rolling after a television interview. The bastards are thought to have included Michael Howard and Michael Portillo.

Critics of Cameron from the left have suggested that his new Conservatism has been no more than a rebranding exercise, and that the party is still fundamentally a Thatcherite Party. Critics from the right feel that Cameron has abandoned too many of the key principles of Thatcher's Party. Which view is correct?

DISCUSSION: HAS CAMERON REALLY CHANGED THE CONSERVATIVE PARTY?

Divide your group in two. One half research the proposition that the party has really only undergone a *rebranding* and its ideological position is essentially unchanged.

The other half should research the proposition that Cameron's conservatism is qualitatively different from conservatisms that have gone before. Both should find evidence to back up their arguments.

Have the debate!

B. Varieties of conservatism

There are a number of key *varieties* of conservatism, developed throughout the history described above.

Traditional Conservatism

Traditional conservatism is the original British conservatism of Burke and the old Tory Party. Central to its values is the idea that Britain did not require any sort of liberal revolution like those that plagued Europe: Britain was already a free society. The freedom of the British people was not secured by some codified constitution but by the nation's traditions and great institutions. As such, protecting those institutions was key to traditional conservatism: nation (and the Union), monarch, aristocracy, Church of England, Parliament, the rule of law: these were the guarantors of freedom. At the same time, this freedom was under threat from rampant industrialism and the foreign liberal ideas that came from the French Revolution.

Traditional conservatives had a particular understanding of *human nature*. While liberals see humans as fundamentally rational, traditional conservatives believe the masses to be fundamentally irrational and in need of leadership: hierarchy, authority and leadership are therefore essential.

While traditional conservatism is generally used to refer to the ideas of Tories in the late 18th and early 19th century, elements of traditional conservatism can still be seen in the modern Conservative Party. The party has always been keen to be the most Royalist of the British parties; it is the most unionist of the parties (now demonstrated by its current pact with the Ulster Unionist Party in Northern Ireland). The nationalism that underlies conservative euroscepticism is also indicative of traditional conservative ideology, and the argument is often couched in the terms of traditional conservatism.

KEY QUOTATION: JOHN MAJOR'S "OLD MAIDS" SPEECH

"Fifty years from now, Britain will still be the country of long shadows on cricket grounds, warm beer, invincible green suburbs, dog lovers and pools fillers and, as George Orwell said, 'Old maids bicycling to holy communion through the morning mist' and, if we get our way, Shakespeare will still be read even in school."

How does John Major's quotation from the 1990s fit in with conservative ideology? How might the Conservative view of Britishness have contributed to their poor performance in elections outside England?

One Nation Conservatism

One nation conservatism developed from one particular thread of traditional conservatism: paternalism. Despite the fundamental importance of hierarchy and elitism within traditional conservatism, there was a belief that the "better" people in society had a *duty* to look after the deserving of the "lower types" of people. It is from that logic that some traditional conservatives were key figures in campaigns for a shorter working week, against child labour and against the slave trade.

Furthermore, the conservative fear of revolution and violent change led many conservatives to be understandably concerned about the massive inequalities of 19th century Britain. Conservatives did not disapprove of inequality – it was inevitable and even desirable – but a nation that had within it very great wealth and dreadful levels of absolute poverty was not a stable nation

These two influences – a paternalistic desire to help the poor and a fear that poverty might lead to revolution and violent change – were key to Disraeli's concerns about the "two nations" of Britain (the rich and the poor). It gave rise to a type of conservatism that saw alleviating poverty as a key part of its mission.

Arguably, it is this one nation strand of conservatism that was to the fore during the long post-war consensus, when conservatives maintained the welfare state, the National Health Service, etc. Some would argue that there is further evidence of one nationism in the modern Conservative Party's dedication to the NHS and its discourse about poverty and social exclusion. However, others would point to the *policies* of the modern Conservative Party in the coalition government and question whether they differed very greatly from the ideas of the New Right Conservative Party of the 1980s, suggesting that only the discourse (and hence the brand) had changed.

New Right

Greatly influenced by the libertarian ideas of Hyeck, and the monetarist economics of Milton Friedman, the New Right represented quite a *radical* political creed, adopted by the Conservative Party in the 1970s and 1980s and also highly influential in the Republican Party in the USA, particularly through Ronald Reagan. It sought to bring an end to the post-war consensus and was based on two ideas: neo-liberalism and neo-conservatism.

Neo-liberalism described the economic agenda of the New Right: laissez-faire, free market capitalism and monetarism. These were not new ideas to the political right. Conservative governments in the 1930s (for example) were strongly committed to a laissez-faire approach to the economy, in the face of economic depression. The Republican, Hoover, took a not dissimilar approach in the USA. In the 1970s and 80s however, this fundamental belief in free markets and small government became much more clearly ideological.

Thatcher and Reagan – courtesy Ronald Reagan Library

Neo-conservatism, on the other hand, brought back elements of traditional conservatism in a modern setting: a strong commitment to traditional values and a rejection of the "permissive" liberal ideology of the 1960s, a strong approach to law and order and a belief in traditional approaches to education, etc. On the international stage, this neo-conservatism also included a virulent anti-communism. It was this radical mix of neo-liberalism and neo-conservatism that drove the governments of Thatcher in the UK and Reagan in the USA.

The modern Conservative Party clearly still has elements of New Right ideology at its heart. The Party's response and attitude to the recent economic crises shows a continued commitment to neo-liberal economics, while the Party appears to maintain a neo-conservative attitude in terms of education, foreign policy and other areas. David Cameron's speeches following the 2011 August riots were particularly neo-conservative in his comments about broken families, lack of discipline, etc.

THE BIG SOCIETY: A NEW NAME FOR THE NEW RIGHT?

Margaret Thatcher once said that there was no such thing as society, whereas David Cameron has said that "there is such a thing as society, but it is not the same thing as the state". Despite the apparent contradiction, the actual key point that both were making is remarkably similar.

The argument was that people shouldn't look to the state to solve their problems, but should take responsibility for it themselves. The key difference appears to be that Thatcher talked about "individuals and their families" whereas David Cameron appears to have added "community" to that list. Otherwise, the central argument is the same: Thatcher focused on the small state while Cameron has focused on what would step in to do the job of the state. Both concepts are essentially New Right ones.

IS THE BIG SOCIETY HAPPENING? GIVE REASONS FOR YOUR ANSWER

Modern Conservatism

The big question, that we have posed periodically throughout this section, is: does the modern conservatism, that David Cameron talks about, represent a new "type" of conservatism? Perhaps it is too early to say.

We have identified ways in which elements of one nation conservatism, New Right ideas and even traditional conservatism can be seen in the modern Conservative Party. David Cameron made a speech in 2009 to his party conference that was *deeply* ideological. In many ways it was a classic exposition of the New Right ideology, combined with a great desire to distance his party from the "nasty party" tag that it had acquired.

CAMERON'S CONSERVATISM: VIDEO

Follow the link from the A2 Ideologies website to "Cameron's Conservatism: Video".

Carefully analyse the (quite long) speech in terms of its ideological content. Make a list of ideas that clearly come under the heading of one or other type of conservatism, and a list of ideas that don't seem to fit anywhere. Discuss the latter list with colleagues: are these unique elements of Cameron's Conservatism or are there places they could go in the conservatisms that have gone before?

C. Conservatism and contemporary party politics

While conservatism is clearly associated with the Conservative Party, the ideology has been deeply influential on other parties in UK politics. The success of Margaret Thatcher in the 1980s arguably led to other parties embracing elements of the New Right ideology in order to get votes.

So just how *conservative* are the main UK political parties?

The Conservative Party

We have discussed at some length in this section the ways in which the different variations of conservatism are apparent in the modern Conservative Party and, as such, these arguments don't need rehearsing here. However, we might briefly consider socio-economic background. The original traditional conservatives were, of course, primarily aristocratic. Since the middle of the 20th century, the Conservative Party has preferred commoners to lead the party and, if anything, has been rather embarrassed of its aristocratic roots. A key element of the New Right ideology was that of the self-made man or woman; a *meritocratic* idea that, in a free market, New Right society, entrepreneurs from any background could make a fortune. While Labour were led by the "public school boy" Tony Blair, most modern Conservative leaders had been state educated (often at grammar schools) and had come from middle-class backgrounds.

When the Conservative Party chose David Cameron as their leader, and rejected David Davies, it represented quite a major change in this trend. Davies was from a working-class background, educated at a secondary modern school; he was almost the living embodiment of the Thatcherite ideas he holds dear. Cameron, on the other hand, was an Old Etonian with aristocratic connections. Although he, too, had a reputation for being a Thatcherite, he fought the leadership election on a more "caring conservatism" prospectus.

Cameron's cabinet is remarkably dominated by public school educated men. Even having to have Liberal Democrats in the cabinet has failed to have much impact on that – Nick Clegg was educated at Westminster School for instance.

Although social class itself is not a necessary indicator of ideology (Tony Benn also went to Westminster School) Cameron and Osborne's associations with the Bullingdon Club and their family fortunes do appear to connect them with a much older type of conservatism than that of Margaret Thatcher or John Major.

The Labour Party

One would assume that there would be precious little evidence of *conservatism* in the Labour Party. However, there are two angles to consider here that might raise doubts over this assertion. One is the undoubted New Right influences on New Labour. The other is the new idea of "Blue Labour".

The Labour Party, in the 1980s and early 1990s started to worry that they might not be able to win a General Election again. I recall being set an essay question, "Must Labour Lose?" at university (probably only three years before 1997! I'm glad I answered that they musn't!) Interestingly, it was the 1992 General Election that did seem to encourage these sorts of questions. In 1992 the Conservative government was unpopular. There had been riots over the poll tax, the Conservative cabinet had got rid of Margaret Thatcher and replaced her with Major (who was seen as uncharismatic and grey). At the same time, Labour seemed to have managed to put the acrimonious infighting of the 1980s behind it, had a fresh-faced team with the likes of Tony Blair and Gordon Brown emerging, alongside more experienced people like John Smith, Margaret Beckett and Kinnock himself. Labour were *very* confident that they would win in 1992. They lost.

The *Sun* had run with the front page "If Labour win will the last person in Britain turn out the light?" and, the next day, "It was the Sun What Won it!" The Conservative Party had successfully presented the, now very moderate, Labour Party as one that was going to greatly raise taxes. The young modernisers in that Shadow Cabinet, along with their friends, were determined that Labour needed to convince people that they had changed for good, and they needed to persuade some of the popular newspapers in Britain, preferably the *Sun*, to get behind them. To do that, they needed to embrace some of the ideology of Margaret Thatcher.

The Labour Left would argue that they had already begun doing that; they would point to Kinnock's decision not to back the miners in the Miners' Strike of 1984/5 as the beginning of the "Thatcherisation" of the Labour Party. By the time of the 1997 General Election, the party was promising not to raise the basic or higher rates of income tax and committing to stick to the spending commitments of the outgoing Conservative Government. Furthermore, they chose not to reverse any of Thatcher's anti-union legislation, did not reverse any of her privatisations and introduced privatisations of their own. After having criticised Conservative governments for their introduction of an "internal market" in the NHS, they went on to introduce market forces in healthcare, education and wherever they could. New Labour was also concerned that they were seen as being "soft on crime". Blair opted for the "tough on crime, tough on the causes of crime" slogan, as such bringing in a more conservative element to this area of policy.

Since Labour lost the 2010 election, there has been something of a battle for its ideological future and one suggested direction has been "Blue Labour". This might be best described as "very old" or "ancient" Labour (as opposed to the radical left "Old Labour"). The Blue Labour case is that many of Labour's traditional working-class voters are inherently conservative. This does not mean that they support modern Conservative policies of privatisation and free markets (although Blue Labour has no particular attachment to public ownership) but more in relation to social attitudes.

> ### WEB RESEARCH: BLUE LABOUR
>
> Have a read of the Blue Labour blog. Are these proposed ideas *conservative* and if so, what type of conservatism do they most resemble? Can they be described as socialist at all?

The Liberal Democrats

The Orange Book Liberals would insist that their support for economic liberalism was inspired not by New Right conservatism, but by classical liberalism. It has to be said that the Orange Bookers pushed for this change in Liberal Democrat policy at a time when the Conservative Party had lost successive elections and therefore, you would imagine, were less influential than in the 1980s and 1990s. Indeed, at a time when Labour was apparently losing lots of its traditional voters, the Liberal

Democrats might have seen electoral advantage in becoming more clearly a party of the *left* and underlining their *social democratic* ideas. Clearly their role as an alternative to Labour had won them considerable victories in local government in many northern cities. They lost these gains in May 2011 after a year in the coalition government.

Of course, some things the Liberal Democrats have done since May 2010 are clearly conservative, but these could have been done simply because they are in a coalition with the Conservative Party rather than because they have adopted elements of the conservative ideology.

ACTIVITY: LIBERAL DEMOCRAT PARTY POLICY TODAY

Go onto the Liberal Democrat Party's website (http://www.libdems.org.uk) and find a handful of their current, bang up-to-date policies. On no more than one sheet of A4 for each policy, analyse them in terms of their *conservatism*. Remember to consider whether *all* conservatives would approve or disapprove of the policy in question and why.

D. Answering exam questions on conservatism

Refer back to the "Liberalism" section for general instructions on answering 10 mark and 30 mark questions.

Topic 3   **Conservatism**

01   How does New Right conservatism differ from traditional conservatism? (10 marks)

The conservatism of the New Right, exemplified by the Thatcher government in the UK and the Reagan presidency in the USA, differs in a number of key ways from traditional conservatism, although there are also some important similarities.

Traditional conservatism is based on the idea that freedom is guaranteed by key traditions: hierarchy, aristocracy, monarchy, parliament, the Church, law and order, patriotism, etc. Humans are not naturally rational, and require the guidance and leadership of "the best" people in society. At the same time, there are responsibilities incumbent upon those leaders to ensure that people are protected and looked after (the paternalistic element of traditional conservatism that informed the "softer" one nation conservatism of Disraeli and 20th century Tory "wets").

This approach led to traditional conservatism often preferring economic protectionism to free trade, as they believed their own country should come first. It also inspired a degree of paternalistic concern for the welfare of the poorest people in society (certainly, at least, the "deserving poor").

The New Right then, were entirely different. Their neoliberal economic agenda always prefers a laissez-faire, free market approach. This did, at times, mean a very radical agenda, undermining traditions and institutions. Neoliberalism also meant that New Right thinkers would prefer self-help to any sort of paternalistic philanthropy. New Right thinkers see human nature as rational and self-interested.

However, the New Right is also based on neoconservatism; here an emphasis on law and order, respect and so-called "Victorian values" is more in keeping with traditional conservative ideas. As such, there is a conservative root to the New Right that stops it from being something wholly alien to conservative traditions.

A different sort of ten mark question might be:

Topic 3	Conservatism
01	Why is conservatism sometimes described as *pragmatic* rather than ideological? (10 marks)

Some have argued (not least some conservatives themselves) that conservatism is not really an ideology at all. (Republican Pat Buchanan, for example, has said "Conservatism is not an ideology". This argument would suggest instead that conservatism is *pragmatic*; conservatives will take the action that will work, rather than that which fits into a predetermined set of ideas or dogma.

This is argued both as a defence of conservatism and as a criticism. As a defence, it suggests that conservatives are not guided by a dogmatic faith but by a detached, pragmatic determination to do what will work: as such, they are more open-minded and flexible than socialists, liberals and the like. As a criticism, it suggests that conservatives do not base their ideas and actions on a set of principles and beliefs but, instead are opportunistic, guided by wanting power or supporting certain interests in society, rather than by principles.

This is often used as an explanation as to why different types of conservatism are so *very* different from one another (e.g. one nation conservatism and New Right conservatism, although it should be noted that different types of liberalism are similarly very different). Although there do appear to be examples of conservatives being pragmatic (e.g. the conservative acceptance of the Welfare State and some nationalisation in the post-war consensus), Margaret Thatcher's New Right conservative government is generally considered to be a *highly* ideological government; and strong commitment to certain right-wing principles seemed to hamper the Conservative Party's return to power after their 1997 defeat, when something more pragmatic could have been attempted. Even David Cameron (whose "modern conservatism" and rebranding of the party could be seen as a good example of conservative pragmatism) has made some

Topic 3	Conservatism
02	To what extent has the ideology of the Conservative Party changed since 1997? (30 marks)

Turn to the model answer plans at the back of the book after you have attempted this question, as with other 30 mark questions

E. Conservativism Glossary

Authoritarianism

Traditional conservatism is essentially an *authoritarian* ideology. It argues that those who are ordained to rule (the *elite*, the *aristocracy*) need to assert their authority and keep other members of society in line. Although this seems to contradict the neo-liberalism of later forms of conservatism, it does seems that economic liberalism can and does go hand in hand with authoritarianism in other fields (e.g. the Thatcher government's authoritarian approach to the miners' union)

Economic Liberalism

Modern conservatives tend to be economically liberal. This is most associated with the New Right ideas of Margaret Thatcher's government, but actually *laissez-faire* economics have often been at the heart of conservatism (despite some periods of conservative *protectionism*)

Elite

Traditional conservatives believe there is an elite group in society: some people are better than others – equality is neither desirable nor possible. For traditional British conservatives this elite was the *aristocracy*.

Hierarchy

Traditional conservatives believe that there is a natural hierarchy in society that everybody should accept. They traditionally believed in the *monarchy* and the important place of the *aristocracy*. Modern conservatives tend to put forward the case for a *meritocracy* although their critics on the left would claim that this was *just ideology* and that they used meritocratic arguments to justify hierarchy (and oppose equality of outcome).

Inequality

Most conservatives believe that inequality is *natural* and *inevitable*. There are a variety of responses to that, with one nation conservatives, for example, feeling that the state has a responsibility to ameliorate the harsh conditions of the poor. Some conservatives would go so far as to suggest that inequality was a positive good as competition provided people with incentives: equality of outcome would take away the incentive to work hard and to try and succeed.

Individualism

Modern conservatism is, like liberalism, and individualistic ideology. Traditional conservatism was rather more concerned about groups and collectives, albeit from an *elitist* and *hierarchical* perspective. However, the modern Conservative Party, under David Cameron, has become interested in *communities* and society, particularly within David Cameron's "Big Society" idea.

Libertarianism

Some of the neo-liberals on the New Right consider themselves to be *libertarians*. These take the principles of minimal government to their logical extremes seeing virtually no legitimate role for a state at all. The most extreme form of this libertarianism is described as "anarcho-capitalism".

Mixed Economy

For a long time after the Second World War and before the leadership of Margaret Thatcher, the British Conservative Party believed in a *mixed economy* (as did the Labour and Liberal parties). This period of *consensus* was brought to a sudden end by Thatcher's belief in *privatisation* and opposition to public ownership. A mixed economy is one where there is a mixture of public and private ownership.

Nationalism

Nationalism has always been a key element of conservatism in Britain. Nationalism can be a radical or revolutionary ideology where a nation is under threat or under occupation, or nationhood is denied; however, in a strong and powerful nation like the United Kingdom, nationalism is a conservative idea, protecting the nation from perceived threats (e.g. anti-colonial campaigns or the European Union) and, at times, asserting the *superiority* of one nation over others.

Organic Society

Conservatives tend to believe in an *organic* society, where change happens gradually and naturally. They see society as a delicate organism where tinkering with one part of society might lead to unintended consequences in another. Of course, Margaret Thatcher once said of society, "there is no such thing!"

Paternalism

Traditional conservatives certainly, and "one nation" and "wet" conservatives quite possibly, can be described as "paternalistic": seeing themselves as a *father* to the lower orders in society and, from that position, perceiving a duty of care towards them. This is seen as an explanation for some traditional conservatives strong opposition to slave trade or child labour, for example.

Pragmatism

Many have questioned whether conservatism should really be considered an ideology *at all*, including many conservatives. Some suggest that it is, instead, *pragmatic*. It tries to find what works, irrespective of a core set of ideas.

This can be viewed positively (i.e. they approach things on a case-by-case basis, not blinded by dogma, etc.) or negatively (i.e. they have no principles and are simply self-serving).

Privatisation

One important element of the neo-liberalism of the modern Conservative Party has been a belief that private companies are better than state providers at providing goods and services. This was put into practice by the Thatcher government that set about privatising most public utilities. These privatisations have not been reversed by Labour governments.

Protectionism

While, certainly in their recent history, the Conservative Party has taken a neo-liberal approach to economic and, as such, has favoured "free trade", there have been periods in the 19th and early 20th century where the Conservatives have preferred *protectionism* or *tariff reform* where they have argued for tariffs and taxes that would support British exports and would be unfavourable towards imports.

FASCISM

A. Historical context

At first glance, it might appear that fascism came from nowhere in 1920s Italy. But, as a variety of *ultra-conservatism*, it could be argued that its roots share the same soil as some forms of traditional conservatism.

Like conservatism, fascism is a *reaction*: it is a reaction to industrialisation, the Enlightenment, liberalism and to socialism. It sees all of these processes as ones that will endanger *nationalism* and the strength of the nation.

Ironically, then, the person who is credited with inventing fascism had his political roots in socialism. Benito Mussolini was a maverick Italian socialist.

He was, however, virulently opposed to both liberalism and Communism. He saw both as potent threats to Italy. The idea that workers in Italy shared common cause with workers in France (or anywhere else) against bosses in Italy appeared to Mussolini to be especially damaging to the strength and unity of Italy as a nation. Mussolini was not interested in *class* consciousness, but in *national* consciousness. It was this essential element of fascism that led Hitler to call his German fascist party the "National Socialists".

The symbol of Italian fascism was a bundle of sticks. This represented the idea that while a stick on its own is weak and easy to break, a bundle of sticks is strong and won't break. That idea, put simply, sounds quite *socialist*. British Labour Party members have the words on their membership cards "by the strength of our common endeavour we achieve more than we achieve alone". But Mussolini's bundle was not the workers against the bosses, or the poor against the rich; it was Italians against foreign foes. It was an essential element of fascism that representatives of the workers and representatives of the owners and bosses were all part of that bundle. What tied them together and united them was obedience to the leader. Finally, and crucially, this bundle (based on a weapon of Ancient Rome called the *fasces*) had an axe's head: fascism was violent.

A key part of Mussolini's fascism was an opposition to *reason*. "Think with your blood!" ran one famous fascist slogan, meaning that people should follow their instincts and passion. Emotions, like nationalism, patriotism, pride, shame and loyalty were more powerful than rationalism.

Although there were *ultra-conservative* movements elsewhere (such as France) which had many similarities with Italian fascism, the other country that clearly came under fascist control in the inter-war years was Germany.

Like Mussolini, Hitler saw a country divided and emasculated. For Hitler, Germany had been emasculated by the "international community" after the First World War, but it was divided by internal enemies. Some of these were the same as Mussolini's internal enemies (Communists and Trade Unionists) but Hitler's fascism had a distinctly racial element. The sticks in Hitler's bundle all had to be "Aryan" and people of other races (e.g. Jews and gypsies) were as much a threat to German unity as the foreign ideas of Communism and liberalism. Hitler and his supporters even argued that Communism was a global Jewish conspiracy (based on little more than the German Jewish heritage of Karl Marx, and the Jewish background of a handful of the original Russian Bolsheviks, such as Leon Trotsky). Another aspect of this fundamental racist element of Hitler's fascism was the idea that the German nation was not the country as it currently appeared on the map, but all Germanic people (whether they liked it or not!)

Not that Mussolini required that justification for also having *imperial* ambitions. Mussolini's idea of Italy was based on ancient Rome, and, like the ancient Romans, he wished to build an Italian *Empire*. Both fascist nations, then, embarked on imperial adventures, both for national glory, demonstrations of military strength and to find "lebensraum" (room to live). Of course, imperialism and Empire were not unique to fascists: the UK still had an enormous empire in the inter-war years, and liberals and conservatives (and even some socialists) had managed to conjure up justifications for imperialism, ranging from the paternalistic to the "civilising".

Furthermore, the racial ideas that underpinned Hitler's version of fascism (Nazism) were not unique to the German National Socialist Party. Anti-Semitism was rife throughout Europe. A pseudo-scientific notion of racial hierarchy, based on a fundamental misunderstanding of Darwin, was also commonplace in Europe. Hitler was not alone in believing the Aryan race to be "superior"; what marked him out as unusual was his extreme political agenda that was rooted in these ideas. The anti-Semitic ideas could be found in any European country in the 1930s, the concentration camps and gas chambers could not.

Like Mussolini, the leader of the British Union of Fascists, Oswald Moseley, had been a socialist politician (although he had also been a Conservative). Moseley had been a popular, charismatic MP. When he left the Labour Party to form the New Party, it was seen as a *left-wing* split from the party, though left-wingers like Nye Bevan and Stafford Cripps viewed it with considerable suspicion. They were right to do so; before long the New Party had become the British Union of Fascists, and Moseley their prospective Fuhrer. His "blackshirts", like Mussolini's Brownshirts, were violent thugs and, like Hitler's henchmen, their targets went beyond trade unionists and Communists; they targeted British Jews.

The British Union of Fascists was never more than a violent minority. Fascist organisations in other countries tended to remain similarly marginalised (like the Blueshirts in Ireland, for example). However, there were other fascist victories, such as for Franco in Spain (the victor of the Spanish Civil War).

Moseley was imprisoned during the Second World War as a traitor, but he made an unlikely comeback in the 1950s, protesting against immigration from the Commonwealth. Following the Allied victory in the Second World War, it was in the politics of anti-immigration and racism that most fascists operated, at least in the UK.

British politicians throughout the second half of the Twentieth Century were guilty of "playing the race card" and at times race became a key political issue (surrounding Enoch Powell's 1968 "Rivers of Blood" speech, for example) but the fascist organisations remained on the margins of British political discourse.

The dominant organisation in the 1970s and much of the 1980s was the National Front (an openly neo-Nazi group). From the late 1980s, their position in British politics was replaced by the British National Party, with many key figures moving from the one organisation to the other. (BNP MEP for Yorkshire and the Humber, Andrew Brons, for example, is a former leader of the NF, with a conviction for anti-Semitic violence).

While the National Front was openly Neo-Nazi, the BNP has tried to distance itself from fascist or Nazi symbolism and imagery and its leader denies being a fascist. However, there are clear fascist and Nazi elements to the politics of the BNP, as discussed in Section C.

In other parts of Europe, far right parties have had some electoral success. The National Front in France has been successful and the party of Geert Wilders in Holland has had considerable success. Austria has seen far right parties prosper in elections and the far right is a significant force in Scandinavia. This came horrifically and bloodily to the world's attention in Oslo in 2011, with the bombings and shootings.

Outside Europe, there were other forms of fascism. A number of fascist dictators came to power in South America. Definitively anti-Communist, many acquired the support of US Governments in the Cold War. There are some clear differences from "classic" fascism. Pinochet's fascist government (sometimes described as "ultra-conservative") used many of the classic hallmarks of fascism - military dictatorship, the torture and extermination of opponents, etc. - but it exercised neo-liberal economic policies, not the *corporatism* of the classic fascist states.

Similarly controversial, there has been some debate as to whether either the Arab nationalist regimes (such as Iraq or Syria under Ba'ath Party rule, Gadaffi's Libya or Mubarak's Egypt) or fundamentalist theocratic regimes (like Saudi Arabia, Iran or Taliban-led Afghanistan) should be described as fascist. Critics of the latter regimes sometimes use the term "Islamofascist". As with some of the Latin American examples, there are clear parallels with classical fascism but also some key differences.

B. Varieties of fascism

Fascism

Although fascism has become a very general term, covering the many varieties listed below, and a general term of abuse, it initially had quite a specific political meaning, for Mussolini, who devised it. It is an intensely elitist and hierarchical popular nationalism. It is often defined by what it opposes: it opposes liberalism, rationalism, socialism, communism, class struggle, internationalism and modernity. It aims for national unity (under one leader), national strength against other nations and for military strength and domination.

Nazism

The equation is sometimes put forward: fascism + racism = Nazism. Although most fascist regimes and parties throughout history appear to have had some racial elements to their aggressive nationalism, racism is absolutely central to Nazism. The national community is defined by *race*. The word Nazism is a contraction of National Socialism, which was Hitler's version of fascism. The ideas are essentially the same, but Hitler's *nationalism* was entirely and definitively a racist one.

Ultra-conservatism

Some organisations and governments that have been linked with fascism are sometimes described as "ultra-conservative". This is often the case if the group is closely linked to the traditionally wealthy or dominant class or group in society, or if there is any royalist or aristocratic element. (Fascism manages to be both a conservative and a *revolutionary* ideology; ultra-conservatism would tend not to be revolutionary). However, "ultra-conservative" is also used to describe otherwise fascist regimes that lasted and had some support from otherwise liberal regimes! Franco in Spain and Pinochet in Chile both acquired this description, seemingly with little more justification than having the support of some foreign conservatives.

There were ultra-conservatives in Germany, Italy and Vichy France who helped to give support and ideological cover for fascism.

Neo-Nazism

Neo-Nazism is the definitively racist fascist politics that can be seen in contemporary Europe and America. While it is particularly associated with pro-Hitler skinheads in Germany and Eastern Europe, its influence can be seen in apparently more "moderate" groups in the UK, France, Sweden, Norway, etc. (some of which have had some electoral success) and is also the ideology of the modern Klu Klux Klan in the USA.

C. Fascism and contemporary politics

Fascism has become such a general term of political abuse that no modern parties (save for a few very fringe neo-Nazi organisations) would self-define as fascist. This does make this section more difficult. It is uncontroversial to consider the Labour Party when discussing socialism, the Liberal Democrats when discussing liberalism and the Conservatives when considering conservatism. To go straight to the BNP and the EDL when discussing fascism is problematic, as both organisations have denied being fascist.

However, if it looks like a duck, walks like a duck, etc, etc.

In many ways the BNP are a classically fascist party, although their preoccupation with race also opens them up to the charge of being a *neo-Nazi* organisation.

Secret filming of BNP events has shown members greeting each other with Nazi salutes, etc. but it is in public statements that most of the party's neo-Nazi elements can be seen:

Leader, Griffin, has described the holocaust as the "holo-hoax". When asked if he had ever denied the holocaust, on BBC Question Time, he replied that he did not have a *conviction* for holocaust-denial. He did say on that programme that he had changed his mind and now believed that the holocaust did happen. A leading member of the BNP condemned Winston Churchill for "betraying his race" (i.e. fighting against Nazi Germany). However, the party routinely uses British military imagery (including from the Second World War) in its publicity, again tying in with the martial imagery of classical fascism. There is no democratic procedure for removing the BNP's party leader and, until a recent rule-change because their constitution was illegal, "non-white" people were barred from party membership.

Other traditional victims of the Nazis are the victims of the BNP's aggression, including gay people (Griffin condemned protestors against the murderous Soho pub bombing of 1999 for "flaunting their perversion"). He did not withdraw his statement, even after it became clear that the murderer (guilty of a string of nail bombs in the capital) was one of his own party members.

The BNP's high point came when Griffin himself and former National Front leader Andrew Brons were elected to the European Parliament. Since then, and a disastrous television appearance by Griffin on BBC Question Time, the party appears to have lost considerable ground. Many of their supporters seem to have abandoned electoral politics and attached themselves to the pressure group, EDL. The EDL claims to have a very specific "anti-terrorist" / anti-fundamentalist Islam agenda, although the targets of their communications and activism appear considerably broader. There is undoubtedly a significant neo-Nazi element in the EDL, and its marches and protests clearly attract this element.

WEB ACTIVITY: THE BNP & FASCISM

Hold your nose and go to the BNP's website (warning – although the party tends to avoid deeply offensive material in its public communications, there may be offensive material on this website, especially on any associated public forums, etc – don't "register" or give any personal details to this site). Find a list of the party's current policies and analyse them in terms of their *fascism* and *Nazism*.

Can you see any elements of other ideologies in the policies?

But are there any elements of fascism in the main UK political parties? Clearly any apparent fascistic elements need to be viewed in the context of all three main UK parties condemning fascism and racism in the strongest possible terms.

Fascism in the Labour Party?

There is a strong tradition of anti-racism and anti-fascism on the left of British politics and many Labour politicians were active in anti-fascist groups in their student days. Could any aspects of Labour Party politics be seen as fascist?

The economic policies of the Wilson and Callaghan governments in the 1970s (and, actually, the Conservative Heath government to some extent too) have sometimes been described as "neo-corporatist". Of course, corporatism is the economic policy of classical fascism. Under these 1970s governments, the CBI and the TUC (the representatives of Capital and Labour) would work with the government on various aspects of economic policy, seeking general agreement in "smoke-filled rooms" with "beer and sandwiches" at Number 10.

SYNOPTIC LINK TO AS – INSIDER GROUPS

During the 1970s, the CBI and the TUC were classic examples of *insider pressure groups*. The CBI would represent the interests of the owners of industries (the bosses) while the TUC would represent the workers in trade unions. Through meetings and committees, important decisions would be taken, including policies on incomes and wages. This situation was criticised from the New Right as stifling the free market, but also from the Left as being corporatist, disarming the trade unions by bringing them into the establishment. The New Right thought that the unions had too strong a role in government, while the "New Left" thought that the bosses were getting too big a say in a Labour government.

However, this apparent similarity might be partly due to fascism's claim to offer a "third way" – not Communism or free-market capitalism. The idea that apparently competing groups (such as workers and bosses) actually have shared interests, and pursuing these interests is in the national interest, is apparent in quite a lot of social democratic thinking. Tony Blair talked of a Third Way himself. It is quite a stretch of the imagination to make any real link between this and fascism other than a semantic one. While some Communists in the 1930s called social democrats "social fascists", it was never a charge that stood up to a great deal of scrutiny!

Critics of the Blair and Brown governments might point to the "illiberal" anti-terror policies, detention without charge, etc. as well as the use of military power to pursue political ends. However, once again, any use of the term "fascist" to describe these governments would really be the use of the term as generalised abuse, or simply as "illiberal", rather than having much to do with the ideology of fascism.

Fascism and the Conservative Party?

Again, any parallels identified here need to be taken with a great big pinch of salt. The Conservative Party did acquire an image as "the nasty party" in the post-Thatcher era, which David Cameron was determined to shake. Part of that image related to what some saw as an unhealthy preoccupation with issues relating to immigration and asylum. The 2005 Conservative Party General Election campaign was strongly criticised for its use of populist innuendo. The slogan "Are You Thinking What We're Thinking?" was certainly a clever one. People thinking a whole range of different things might well have assumed that the Conservative Party was indeed thinking the same as them (although they still lost the election, so perhaps not!) Without resorting to making any hugely controversial statements, it was felt that the slogan sometimes referred to race and immigration. While then leader Michael Howard was himself the child of refugees, there was a good deal of disquiet about the campaign, which had a major influence on David Cameron and what he chose *not* to talk about in his campaigns.

The Conservative Party's euroscepticism has found them consorting with some curious bedfellows in the European Parliament. Most centre-right parties in Europe are part of the European People's Party, but that is a passionately europhile party (the centre right in Europe is predominantly europhile, while the hard left tends to be more eurosceptic). As such, the Conservative Party has made links with right-wing eurosceptic parties in the EU Parliament in the European Conservatives and Reformists group, some of which have been accused of being associated with fascism.

While some might point to the militarism and jingoism of the Thatcher government in the Falklands conflict as smacking of fascist militarism, others might fairly point out that the conflict was against a fascist regime in Argentina.

It is the race issue that presents itself as the most likely reason to associate some moments in the history of the Conservative Party with fascist ideology (along with them both being ideologies of the "right", with all the difficulties and problems such terminology brings!) Conservative MP, Enoch Powell's famous "Rivers of Blood" speech of 1968 unveiled a thread of Conservative opinion that saw ethnic diversity in the UK as a problem. In completely different terms and in a completely different context, David Cameron attacked "state-sponsored multiculturalism" sparking some criticism as well as support. While it is much easier to defend the motivation behind the second speech than the first one, some have argued that although Enoch Powell's arguments helped the arguments of racists, he himself was not a racist. That is an argument that might never be satisfactorily resolved. Less open for debate is the Conservative Party local leaflet from the 1964 General Election where the candidate for Smethwick, Peter Griffiths, used the slogan "if you want a nigger for a neighbour, vote Liberal or Labour". However, all parties will have had some racist members, as racism is sadly still quite common in society, and used to be rife; while the Conservative Party perhaps has a bigger historical "problem" with race, it would be absurd to extrapolate from that any relationship with fascism or Nazism.

Fascism and the Liberal Democrat Party?

Because fascism is seen by some to be the very opposite of liberalism, it would be surprising to find even the most vague and spurious connections between fascism and the Liberal Democrat Party. However, the use of the word "liberal" is not an antidote to fascism in itself! - the Russian Liberal Democrat Party is a "far right" ultranationalist (and some would argue neo-fascist) party!

Perhaps the only way in which some sort of argument along these lines could be constructed would be in the area of populist opportunism (although all parties have been guilty of that from time to time!)

One reason why it is quite hard to accurately define and delineate the fascist ideology is that fascists use populist ideas to gain power, but do not necessarily *believe* everything they say. This is a charge that has, on occasion, been levelled at the Liberal Democrat Party – fairly or otherwise. It has been suggested that the party will present itself as being to the left in the North of England and to the right in the South of England, for example (depending on who they intend to gain votes from). This is poor electioneering if found out, but hardly fascist! More concerning, in some local elections in the 1990s, the Liberal Democrats were accused of "playing the race card" in their leaflets. Similarly, prejudice appears to have been central to the Bermondsey by-election Liberal Democrat leaflets that called on voters to "make the straight choice" rather than vote for Labour candidate and gay rights campaigner, Peter Tatchell.

However, as with the Labour and Conservative Parties, there is no convincing case to be made. Fascism is a peculiar and singular ideology, based on a rejection of reason and of other ideologies, so it is not surprising to find it confined to the far right-wing fringe of British politics today.

D. Answering exam questions on fascism

For general information about answering ten-mark questions, see the part (d) of the Liberalism section.

Again, ten-mark questions on fascism are likely to take one or other of these general forms, the "compare and contrast" or the "contextualisation".

Topic 4
01   Explain the difference between fascism and Nazism (10 marks)

So, we explain both terms and pick out key differences.

For some, there is no real difference between fascism and Nazism. Nazism merely refers to one particular example of fascism, in Germany in the 1930s. Others would argue that Nazism has some particular features that differentiate it from other forms of fascism.

Fascism is a type of extreme populist, elitist nationalism that developed in Italy in the 1920s and influenced a small number of governments and numerous movements in the 20th century and today. Although aggressive nationalism was always at the heart of fascism, an emphasis on *race* was a particular feature of the fascism that took root in 1930s Germany; the ideology of Adolf Hitler and the German National Socialist (Nazi) party. As such, the equation Fascism + Racism = Nazism is sometimes used.

Apart from the preoccupation with race – the pseudo-scientific conclusion that the Aryan race was superior to all others – Nazism was very similar to Italian fascism. Both philosophies were anti-democratic, anti-Communist, anti-liberal, anti-reason and anti-Enlightenment. Both philosophies were intensely nationalistic, put a strong emphasis on the role of the *leader* and aspired towards *totalitarianism* (the involvement of the state in all aspects of national life).

However, racism became a truly central and defining aspect of Nazism, particularly in terms of its anti-Semitism and "final solution" holocaust during the Second World War. Hitler's leadership of the axis powers in the Second World War did lead to racist policies being enacted in Italy too. The British Union of Fascists was strongly influenced by Hitler and anti-Semitism was a key part of their politics, and most fascist movements since the war have been preoccupied with race. It might be, therefore, that they are better described as neo-Nazi movements, or that fascism and Nazism are essentially the same, except for a small number of fascist groups that have had less of a preoccupation with race.

A contextualisation-style question might be:

Topic 4

01   Why do fascist organisations support totalitarianism? (10 marks)

In this question, we need to define the term, and put it firmly in the context of fascist ideology:

Totalitarianism is the idea that the state should involve itself in every aspect of national life. A totalitarian regime would seek to control everything: there would be no "private sphere" away from the eyes of the state, and there would be no *pluralism* where different groups, organisations or individuals might have influence or power over individuals or sections of society.

A totalitarian state might achieve this by limiting or banning some organisations and activities, and also by ensuring all media is directly state-controlled and through the use of secret police or other forms of surveillance.

Some Communist states were described as totalitarian in the 20th century (especially the Soviet Union under Stalin) but fascism is an ideology that actively and openly *supports* totalitarianism: the concept was invented by Mussolini's fascists.

Fascists are specifically interested in the unity, solidarity and power of a nation and see that coming from loyalty and obedience to the state and especially to the *leader*. Puralism and private spheres away from the state are threats to that unity. It is here where alternative influences might erode people's core national identity. Religious and political groups might sow disunity by bringing people into a separate community, either separate within the state, or bringing people together in some sort of international community, both of which undermine the fascist agenda.

It must be pointed out that, while Mussolini aspired to totalitarianism, he did not achieve it. The Catholic Church, for example, remained a potent force in Italy, compromised but not controlled by the state. Nazi Germany was much closer to being a successful totalitarian fascist regime.

The Thirty-mark Question (4)

Topic 4	
02	"Fascism is primarily identified by what it *opposes* rather than what it supports." Discuss (*30 marks*)

After attempting this, turn to the back of the book for a model essay plan.

E. Fascism glossary

Corporatism

Corporatism was the economic policy favoured by fascist parties in the 1920s and 1930s. Its key aim was national unity. It saw conflict between Capital and Labour (stirred up by socialists and communists!) as being contrary to the national interest. Therefore fascists believed that representatives of Capital and Labour should meet, under the auspices of the state, to ensure all work in the national interest and to avoid conflict. As such, private companies were encouraged to remain private, but to work in the state's view of the national interest. Because of the strong links between the unions and socialism (and communism) new, fascist unions had to be created to represent the interests of Labour.

Cult of Personality

Fascism tends to build a "cult of personality" around a leader. Mussolini and Hitler are clear examples of this, but even unsuccessful parties (like the British Union of Fascists) tried to establish popular support for a charismatic leader. Fascists in government would have images of the leader everywhere.

Elites

Like traditional conservatism, fascism is an *elitist* ideology. It is based on the idea that a dominant group in society is *the best* and should lead the rest of society. Democracy and pluralism lead to *weak leadership*. The elite, for fascists, does not have to be an aristocracy (unlike for some European ultra-conservatives) – indeed fascists might be very critical of aristocrats. The elite is simply the top fascists.

Nationalism

Nationalism has proved an essential element of fascism. It is interesting that fascism flourished in the two newest European nations, where nationalism (albeit in a more constructive and liberal form) had been a central and founding principle. Fascist nationalism is aggressive and assertive: like most forms of *conservative* nationalism it is based on a sense of national superiority (even if, ironically, derived from a perception of national inferiority) but for fascists that superiority should be proven on the battlefield. It is a martial (militaristic) ideology.

Nazism

Nazism was the particular form of fascism that was established in Hitler's Germany. A simple formula is: FASCISM + RACISM = NAZISM

As such, most modern fascist organisations, because of the primacy of race within those organisations, are perhaps best described as Nazi or neo-Nazi.

Racism

Racism – discrimination based on race, skin colour or other associated characteristics – has long been associated with the fascist ideology. There are, of course, racists who are not fascists, and it is argued that racism is not an essential element of fascism. It was not central to Mussolini's fascism (although an aggressive nationalism was). Racism is particularly associated with *Nazism*.

Romanticism

It seems strange to apply a word so pleasant-sounding as "romantic" to an ideology so brutal as fascism, but Fascism's rejection of logic and reason and embracing of glory, nation and sacrifice is sometimes seen as a romantic position.

Social Darwinism

While fascists generally rejected many of the "rational" and "reasoned" aspects of the new scientific ideas that emerged from the Age of Reason, some aspects of Darwinism interested fascists: particularly the concept of the *survival of the fittest*. They may or may not have accepted this idea in terms of the origin of species, but instead applied them to society and to nations (in a way that Darwin himself never intended). Fascists therefore would argue that the strongest will always prosper and therefore it is important to be strong – particularly for a nation to be strong.

Totalitarianism

Mussolini, like other fascists that followed him, believed in *totalitarianism*. A totalitarian state is one where the state involves itself in *all aspects* of people's lives. In a totalitarian state, there is no "private sphere" away from the eyes of the state; anything an Italian does is the business of Italy (and therefore the business of Il Duce) for example. It is generally felt that Mussolini failed to establish totalitarianism in Italy, whereas Hitler was more successful in achieving the same in Germany. Interestingly, Stalin's Russia was probably more successful in establishing totalitarianism than most fascist states

PART TWO: POLITICAL ISSUES - IDEOLOGIES IN ACTION

INTRODUCTION TO POLITICAL ISSUES

This module is a very good companion module to the "Ideologies" module, providing students with the opportunity to *apply* their learning from the previous module to some key policy areas.

Those areas are: Ethnicity and Gender, Education, the Economy and the Environment. In each area the student needs to be aware of key issues and debates in the area, key policies and ideas including key legislation and the policies of the main political parties, and the different *ideological* perspectives on these policy areas.

Again, as with the Ideologies module, to tackle the exam the student will need to answer questions from two "topics" – i.e. on *two* of these policy areas, from a choice of four. Again, entering the exam with as much choice as possible is important, but students may well – when revising – decide to abandon one policy area. However, they should be cautious in doing this: it might well be the area that offers the "friendliest" questions on the day.

Because so much of this module relates to current policies, and current policies are constantly changing, this section should be read in conjunction with the A2 Ideologies website.

ETHNICITY & GENDER

A. Key issues

i. Ethnicity

One of the main current issues relating to ethnicity in UK politics is the issue of *multiculturalism*.

Multiculturalism is a much used and abused term. Those who fear that Britain is too culturally diverse, including Prime Minister David Cameron, describe multiculturalism as a well-meaning government agenda that has failed. But it is perhaps more reasonable to describe multiculturalism as an inevitable element of a modern, diverse, pluralistic democracy. The things that the critics focus on – "ghettos", separated communities and separated education – are really examples of the opposite of what people would have traditionally meant by multiculturalism! A multicultural society is one where a variety of cultures, beliefs and ethnicities can peacefully co-exist together – not one where they uneasily co-exist apart.

The historical reasons for ethnic groups to live together in local areas (and, as a consequence of that, local areas and local services such as schools *not* being multicultural) have very little, if anything, to do with a government "experiment". There are "push" and "pull" factors. Immigration was encouraged to certain parts of the country with certain industries (for example the mill towns of northern England) after the War. Existing communities prove a draw for newer immigrants because of issues relating to language, support networks, family and the presence of religious institutions, food, etc. Hostility and racism elsewhere has also been a key factor. The same factors discourage new generations from leaving those areas. The net result is that, in a country that is more than 90% "white British", there are areas that are predominantly African-Caribbean, Asian, Chinese, Jewish, etc. This has nothing to do with successive governments' policies relating to multiculturalism. Indeed it was multicultural "experiments" that led to failed attempts to bus children around cities like Bradford to achieve more "mixed" schools.

The problem, for the critics of multiculturalism, is not so much the existence of "ghettos" but an apparent lack of a shared, British culture. This concern has been expressed by numerous politicians over the years. Norman Tebbit talked about a "cricket test" – which team people support in a Test Match proves where their loyalties lie. The speech was greatly criticised and rightly so: people support sport teams for any number of reasons, and if British Pakistanis choose to support Pakistan against England in the cricket – why not? And, of course, Britain is a diverse country *anyway*. When Andy Murray (the Scottish, British tennis player) commented that he supported whoever happened to be playing against England in football, he caused some outrage, but outrage that was soon forgotten when he was winning tennis games. There seems to be far less concern about people with frankly the vaguest Irish connections supporting Ireland in a rugby match, ex-pat Australians supporting Australia, etc, etc. As such, it is hard to escape the conclusion that skin colour is a factor here.

The issue burst back into the mainstream of political debate in the UK after the 7/7 London bombings. The realisation that the bombers were British muslims, born in Britain, taught in British schools, living and working in British towns, reignited the argument about diversity and the lack of a shared culture. Of course, many IRA bombers had also been born and raised in Britain. So had the far-right nail bomber who terrorised London in 1999. But the issue of *political extremism* became widely connected, in the minds of many, with the issue of multiculturalism and difference.

When France banned the public wearing of niqabs and burkhas, there were calls from some for the UK to follow suit. Others argued that such a ban would be "un-British". The debate about religious dress, particularly those items that cover the face, has been a fascinating one, and one that has divided Islam in Britain. Indeed, one British Imam burned niqabs to illustrate his opposition to them. Calls for bans or restrictions have united those on the political right who believe Geert Wilders' wild prophesies of the "Islamification" of Europe, with feminists, usually on the political left, who view the niqab and the burkha as potent symbols of the oppression of women.

DISCUSSION: DIVERSITY & LIBERALISM

The French government's ban on overtly religious dress is justified
on the basis of France's secular, republican values: in other words,
on its founding liberalism. However, many liberals would argue
that freedom of expression – including freedom of religious
expression in public spaces – is a human right.

In your group, discuss what different types of liberals would say
about this issue. How does it fit in with John Stuart Mill's principles
of liberty? What liberal arguments could be used to justify the
French law?

Those who criticise what David Cameron calls "state-sponsored multiculturalism"
prefer *integration*. In fact, there is no contradiction between multiculturalism and
integration. The counter-argument to the critics of multiculturalism is that they are
not arguing for *integration* but for *assimilation*; they are opposing diversity.

There is a potential problem with wanting everybody to adopt a peculiarly and
specifically British culture. That is, put simply, that nobody seems entirely clear
what British culture is! Is it John Major's cricket, warm beer and old maids? Is it
football, cold lager and fighting? Is it diversity and multiculturalism? Is it empire,
hope and glory? Is it democracy, radicalism and progress? There is no consensus

about what Britishness really means, therefore how could anybody *assimilate* into a British culture?

The really big key issue relating to ethnicity and modern politics is *racism*. Racial discrimination is all too common a feature of world politics, fuelling terrifying events from the "final solution" of Nazi Germany, through Klu Klux Klan lynch mobs in the southern states of the USA, through "ethnic cleansing" in former Yugoslavia, on to modern "far right" horrors, like the 1999 nail bombs in London and the 2011 Oslo bombings and shootings. But as well as Nazi and neo-Nazi movements, racism has been present as a much more day-to-day feature of life in modern societies, and one that several pieces of legislation have attempted to deal with (as discussed in the next section).

Interestingly, Britain had its first minority-ethnic MP in 1922. Shapurji Dorabji Saklatvala ("Comrade Sak") was the Labour MP for North Battersea and an Indian-born member of the Communist Party. Saklatvala served in Parliament until 1929, but there was not another minority-ethnic MP until 1987. In 1987, Keith Vaz, Diane Abbott, Bernie Grant and Paul Boateng were all elected as Labour MPs.

Between 1929 and 1987, there was a great deal of political discussion and debate about race, ethnicity and immigration, but it was a discussion and a debate that did not include black people. Enoch Powell's famous 1968 "Rivers of Blood" speech was strongly criticised by members of the Labour government and it ultimately ended Powell's career as a Conservative MP. But the public discussions about his speech lacked the inevitably valuable contributions that might have been made by black or Asian MPs. Similarly, it was an all-white government and an all-white Parliament that introduced the Race Relations Act in 1976. It is certainly worth remembering the sort of Britain that existed before the Race Relations Act; the sort of Britain where "NO BLACKS, NO IRISH" was a common sight in guesthouse windows.

There was an extraordinary reaction around the world when the USA elected Barack Obama, their first black President. In the context of their turbulent history and the relatively recent fights for civil rights for black Americans, it was a truly remarkable event. However, the prospect of a BAME (black, Asian or minority-ethnic) Prime Minister in the UK seems very distant. In 2010, Diane Abbott became the first BAME candidate for the leadership of a major political party, but she came last in the field of five candidates. The most senior BAME member of the current government is not an elected politician: Baroness Warsi. For all that some British people probably feel some degree of liberal superiority to the US (particularly when looking at the States during the neo-conservative Bush presidency) Colin Powell, Condoleeza Rice and now Barack Obama have scaled heights in the US political system currently out of the reach of BAME politicians in Britain.

The final issues to consider, in relation to race and ethnicity, are those of immigration and asylum. They are undoubtedly related to the other issues; questions about multiculturalism and integration are really questions about immigration, and recent migrants and asylum-seekers have been the victims of racial discrimination.

What do the two terms mean? Immigration is a broad term meaning everybody moving into a country (a subset of *migration*). Asylum-seekers are just one type of immigrant. Throughout history, people have had to leave the country of their birth and seek refuge or asylum somewhere else. In the areas immediately surrounding war-zones (for example) there is often a refugee crisis as huge number of people have to be housed in temporary camps, etc. There is a principle in international law that people fleeing from persecution have a right to claim asylum. There is a media perception that the UK is a "soft touch" and that people attempt to get to the UK rather than other countries. In fact, the UK's approach to asylum-seekers, with the use of detention centres for example, is quite harsh and unwelcoming compared with many European states. A more accurate criticism would be that the system in the UK is inefficient and people often get trapped in the asylum process for long periods of time.

Although it is a myth that the UK takes greatly more than its fair share of asylum seekers compared with other countries, the UK is quite a popular destination because English is such a widely-spoken language. Refugees are also attracted to countries where there are existing communities originating from their country, region or faith background.

Controversy in UK politics has been in relation to so-called "bogus asylum seekers": people who claim to be fleeing persecution in order to be able to get around restrictions on other forms of immigration. David Blunkett (former Labour Home Secretary) controversially argued that Iraqi and Afghan refugees from before those wars should return to their home countries, despite the clear dangers that are still present there.

Some on the political left argue that too much is made of the distinction between fleeing from political persecution and fleeing from extreme poverty. *Economic migration* is seen as being less acceptable or justifiable than asylum-seeking, yet – it is argued – the people might be fleeing emergencies of similar magnitude. Most of us have some economic migrants in our family tree. Others on the centre and left, however, criticise the media for always talking about asylum and *illegal immigration* together, thus creating an association between the two.

In the 2005 general election campaign, the Conservative Party talked about limiting asylum-seekers with a *quota*. This policy was widely criticised as it appeared to fail to take into account the influence of unforeseen events (civil wars, revolutions, etc.) Since then, most political discussion of asylum has focused on improving the *system* and speeding up the application and appeal process, from all parties.

In terms of other immigration, economic migration from within the European Union has been another key area of controversy. One key principle of the European Union has been free movement of labour within its borders. While the difference in wealth between European states was relatively small this was reasonably uncontroversial. With the accession of former communist states, the incentives for migration on quite a large scale became much clearer. As such, the focus of political discourse about immigration shifted to workers from Poland or the Czech Republic, rather than from Commonwealth countries. Controversy surrounding this issue led to Gordon Brown as Prime Minister referring to creating "British jobs for British workers". Although some restrictions on free movement of labour have been put in place for the most recent accessions to the European Union, it is only those parties that favour leaving the European Union entirely (e.g. UKIP and the BNP) that have been able to argue that they would control European immigration. "Tough-sounding" talk from the other parties about immigration controls and Australian-style points systems (limited to non-EU immigration) has alienated some left-leaning and social liberal voters, but has done little to alleviate the concerns of voters for whom controlling immigration is a priority.

ii. Gender

Perhaps the main issue relating to gender and politics is that of *patriarchy* and the struggle against it.

Feminism is fundamental to discussions about the politics of *gender*. Feminism is a broad political movement. Indeed, it is so broad that people often talk about a number of *feminisms* rather than of one coherent perspective or ideology. However, all feminisms share the view that society is *patriarchal* (dominated by men) and that women need to engage in a struggle against patriarchy.

QUICK GUIDE: FEMINISMS

Liberal Feminism This type of feminism focuses on equality before the law. Liberal feminists wish to ensure that men and women have equal opportunities, equal pay, and equal rights to goods, services, jobs, fair treatment, etc. Liberal feminists were encouraged by legislation like the Equal Pay Act and the Sex Discrimination Act and though they would still be concerned about the *gender pay gap* and the *glass ceiling*, they would feel that feminism has been quite a successful movement with many victories.

Radical Feminism Radical feminists on the other hand see changes in the law and the presence of equality policies as being only a very small part of the battle. They see patriarchy as being much more culturally ingrained than that. Men do not only dominate women through law and policy, they do it through the threat of physical violence and through centuries of developing a culture where women expect to be subordinate; even welcome it. There are different levels of radical feminism, but at its most radical, they might propose *separatism*, based on a conclusion that men and women cannot coexist on an equal footing.

Marxist or Socialist Feminism These feminists see patriarchy as being a key problem in society, but it is not the only one. Capitalism is also an evil in society, and its greatest impact is on women. Working-class women are doubly discriminated against – as members of a subordinate, exploited class *and* as members of a subordinate, exploited gender.

Black or Difference Feminism These feminists would add another layer of exploitation to those recognised by the socialist feminists: *ethnicity*. For difference feminists, minority ethnic, working-class women are the most exploited people in society. Multiple discrimination has a massive impact on their lives: gender + class + race

Post-modern Feminism Post-modern feminists argue that women have unprecedented power, choice and opportunity in contemporary society. Their interest is much more in issues of *identity* – a desire to reclaim femininity and the language of femininity; to encourage women to feel empowered and liberated. At its most trivial, this might be the Spice Girl notion of "Girl Power"!

As with ethnicity, an interesting case study for looking at the extent and limits of equality is British politics.

As soon as women got the vote (1918 for well-off, mature women) some began to play key roles in front-line politics. There had been senior women in political organisations before this, but they could not stand for election, or indeed vote in elections. In 1918, Constance Markievicz was elected as Britain's first female MP. However, as a Sinn Fein MP, opposed to the Westminster parliament's authority over Ireland, she never took her seat. The first woman to take her seat in Parliament was the Conservative, Nancy Astor, elected in 1919. A slow stream of women followed her into parliament, including Margaret Bondfield, the Labour MP who became the first female government minister.

Since those early beginnings, Britain has had one female Prime Minister, Margaret Thatcher. But more than thirty years after the election of Thatcher, there are still remarkably few women in senior positions in British politics.

Before the 1997 General Election, the Labour Party decided to take a radical step to try and address this issue. It introduced an *affirmative action* programme in the selection of its parliamentary candidates: all women shortlists. This system, still used by the Labour Party, ensures that a percentage of winnable seats *must* select a woman to be the Labour Party candidate. It was remarkably successful with a large group of new female MPs (dubbed "Blair's Babes" by the press) elected in 1997. But the approach has always been controversial. Potential male candidates, especially local candidates, have felt unfairly treated by the process. There have been allegations that the process has been targeted politically (i.e. to stop specific male candidates from being selected). Those male Labour members opposed to all women shortlists are inevitably caricatured as sexist dinosaurs.

However, another criticism of the scheme has come from some established female politicians who successfully defeated male opponents to get their seats in parliament. Shouldn't the local parties select the best available candidate – who is likely to often be a woman – rather than just the best available female candidate?

Such an argument sounds convincing, but there is a compelling retort: if gender equality is possible through the old system, why didn't it happen? Why did many women choose not to stand as candidates? Why did local Labour parties often select the best male candidate, rather than the best candidate? From this perspective, affirmative action is a necessary evil – hopefully one day there will be no need for such approaches.

Others have argued for more radical change, such as having two MPs for every constituency, one male and one female. Of course, the counter argument to this is, why do this with gender and not with other social identities? Why not ensure that there is fair representation of different ethnicities, sexualities, social classes, etc. by similar means? For feminists, gender is the fundamental and defining identity, but it isn't for everybody.

The Conservative Party, too, under David Cameron, decided that it needed more female MPs. They had been very critical of all-women shortlists and opted instead for an "A List" of recommended candidates that had a lot of female, minority ethnic and "minor celebrity" names on it. Local parties were not compelled to choose from the A List, but it was clear that these candidates were favoured by the central party. Like all-women shortlists, the A List approach has led to an increase in female Conservative MPs, though not on the same scale as Labour's change in 1997.

B. Key legislation and reform

QUICK GUIDE: UK EQUALITY LEGISLATION RELATING DIRECTLY OR INDIRECTLY TO GENDER OR ETHNICITY

Equal Pay Act (1970) Introduced the concept of equal pay for equal work; men and women had to be paid the same amount for doing the same job (it did *not* eradicate the *gender pay gap. Why not?*)

Sex Discrimination Act (1975) Made it unlawful to treat a man or a woman less favourably on the basis of their sex; this included *pregnancy discrimination*.

Race Relations Act (1976) Made it unlawful to discriminate against someone on the basis of their race, colour, ethnic or national origins

Public Order Act (1986) Among other measures, introduced the offence of "incitement to racial hatred" making it unlawful to publish or distribute materials intended to stir up racial hatred or that is likely to stir up racial hatred.

Human Rights Act (1998) Brought the European Convention on Human Rights into UK law.

Sex Discrimination (Gender Reassignment) Regulations (1999) Extended terms of Sex Discrimination to discrimination re: gender reassignment (only applied to employment and vocational training)

Race Relations (Amendment) Act (2000) Placed a duty on public authorities to *promote* race equality

Equality Act (2010) Previous equality legislation (referring to a wide range of "protected characteristics" not just ethnicity and gender) consolidated in one single law.

Discrimination legislation refers to employment, education and the provision of goods and services unless otherwise stated.

PRINT OUT A SUMMARY OF THE EQUALITY ACT (SEE WEBSITE)

C. Ethnicity, gender and contemporary party politics

ACTIVITY: UP-TO-DATE POLICIES

Go the websites of each of the three main political parties (there are clear links on the A2 Ideologies accompanying website). For each party, find their key, current policies relating to ethnicity and gender. You are likely to find these policies in sections about *equality* or about *rights* or *communities*. You might also find some gender-related policies in sections relating to *families*.

For each party, analyse their policies about a) ethnicity and b) gender in terms of the underlying *ideologies*

Keep this in your party policy file.

D. Answering exam questions on Ethnicity and Gender

Topic 1	Ethnicity & Gender
01	Explain what is meant by the term "affirmative action" (10 marks)

Clearly part of this answer would be a straightforward definition like that given in the glossary below. To maximise possible marks however, it is a good idea to give an example and contextualise the arguments within that example. In this chapter we talked about all-women shortlists used by the Labour Party and also the "A List" used by the Conservative Party, in relation to the selection of their parliamentary candidates. The Labour Party has also employed a small number of all-BAME shortlists in some London constituencies. These are interesting and contrasting examples of affirmative action that might be used in your answer.

01   What is the difference between *asylum* and *immigration*? (10 marks)

This is a reasonably straightforward *compare and contrast* question:

Although politicians often combine asylum and immigration when discussing these aspects of government policy, asylum-seekers (or refugees) are really just one small sub-set of immigration, and ones with a significantly different status from other immigrants.

Immigration refers to all migration into a country: there are a wide range of reasons why people might wish to migrate, for work, study, family reasons, etc. One reason – fleeing persecution – changes the legal status of the immigrant into that of a *refugee*. While countries can set their own restrictions on other forms of immigration, they have a legal duty under international law (as well as a moral duty) to grant asylum to people fleeing persecution at home. However, governments are wary that people seek to abuse the asylum system in order to get around other restrictions on immigration, therefore it is usual for there to be an investigation into whether a claim is genuine or not.

While that investigation takes place, in the UK, the person is an *asylum seeker* rather than a refugee and there are significant legal restrictions on that person (they cannot seek or obtain employment, for example). Many asylum seekers are kept in detention centres. If a claim is found to be false (and the person therefore considered a *bogus asylum seeker*) then they are deported, although there is often a complex process of appeals.

The UK has a strict "points system" for immigration from non-EU countries. It has a long record of providing asylum to refugees, even from before this was enshrined in international law, although there has also been criticism of UK's asylum procedures (for being inefficient) and controversy surrounding the use of detention centres, especially when families with children are detained.

An important point to remember is that, when you get a question like this, both terms should be properly explained alongside the exploration of the points of comparison.

The Thirty-Mark Question (5)

Topic 1	Ethnicity and Gender
01	"Multiculturalism has failed." Discuss (*30 marks*)

After attempting this question, turn to the back of the book and look at the model answer plan. Use this in the same way as other model answer plans and model answers in the book.

E. Ethnicity and Gender Glossary

Affirmative Action

Affirmative action relates to any action taken to try and redress historic discrimination against certain groups in society. When referred to as "positive discrimination" it tends to suggest people being preferred purely on the basis of their gender, ethnicity, etc, but affirmative action would more commonly refer to exploring different places to advertise jobs, reconsidering the language of advertisements, setting challenging recruitment targets, etc.

Anti-racism

An anti-racist movement has developed in many countries in the world. In the US, it emerged in the Civil Rights movements of the 1960s; in the UK it has focused considerably on racist and fascist organisations (through groups like the Anti-Nazi League, United Against Fascism, etc.) and has tended to have close links with hard left, socialist groups.

Assimilation

Assimilation refers to an approach to immigration where immigrants abandon their native culture, traditions and customs and take on all the culture, traditions and customs of their new country. The idea rather depends on the idea that there *is* a cohesive set of customs and traditions that everybody adheres to in that country.

Asylum

The concept of asylum is an ancient one, and is based on the idea of people fleeing persecution and claiming *asylum* or *refuge* elsewhere. These people then become *refugees*. While most modern democracies see granting asylum as an important aspect of their liberal democracy, it has become a controversial issue in many countries, with arguments raging about "bogus" asylum seekers (ecomomic migrants claiming asylum in order to bypass strict rules on migration).

Discrimination

Discrimination is a word that can be used in many ways. In a positive (or at least "neutral") way, people can be said to discriminate between good and bad music, wine or literature. When discrimination is applied to

people it is clearly *negative* and goes hand in hand with *prejudice*: it is, in this context, *acting* on prejudice and stereotypes.

Equal Opportunities

"Equal Opps" or "Equality and Diversity" tends to relate to those policies and procedures existing in any organisation to attempt to prevent discrimination and prejudice and to deal with them should they arise. Although "equal opportunities" has a clear literal meaning, it has come to be used as a more general catch-all term for anti-discrimination.

Exclusion

Through the 1990s, the language of social *inclusion* and *exclusion* was increasingly used. Social democrats believed everybody should be *included* in society and if people were excluded – whether this be the poor, or some minority ethnic groups, or indeed women from some workplaces – then both those individuals and society in general lost out.

Feminism

Feminism is an ideology or perspective on society that wishes to bring an end to *patriarchy*. Feminists see society as being male-dominated in a variety of ways. There are a number of different kinds of feminists, as discussed in the chapter, including *liberal feminists*, *radical feminists*, *Marxist feminists*, *difference feminists*, *post-modern feminists*, etc.

Gender

Gender is about *identity* and is therefore distinct from *sex* which is about *biology*. Somebody might identify themselves as being female while biologically being male. This suggests that there are clear *cultural* differences between men and women.

Immigration

Immigration simply refers to people moving into a country. There might be all sorts of reasons why people do this, and most countries have laws restricting immigration (therefore leading to the concept of *illegal immigration*). One reason for immigration might be asylum, others might be economic (to find work), educational, family-related, etc. *Immigration* specifically refers to people coming *into* a country, *emigration* is leaving and *migration* refers to any coming and going around the world.

Integration

Presented by critics of "multiculturalism" as its opposite, although there is not really any contradiction between the two, integration (in the context of race and ethnicity) refers to people from different ethnic backgrounds living together, working together, as part of a cohesive community rather than as isolated or "ghettoized" communities.

Multiculturalism

Multiculturalism is a much used and abused term. It is really a term used to describe a diverse society – one in which there are a number of cultures. (It is hard to imagine a unicultural society – even fascist totalitarians probably failed to produce such a thing!) It has come to be used to describe a society where different ethnic groups co-exist with little or no *integration*. As such it is sometimes referred to as a "project" that has "failed" rather than just the reality of a modern, diverse society.

Patriarchy

Patriarchy is a term used by feminists to describe a society dominated by men.

Political Correctness

Political correctness (often shortened to PC) is a term used (normally in a negative, pejorative sense) for attempts to try and eliminate language that might be offensive from public discourse. Letter-writers and columnists in the popular press often feel that political correctness has "gone mad" and clearly at times this difficult area has been handled clumsily by some organisations and local councils. There is clearly a Millian liberal argument to be had here: does one person's

right to free speech trump other people's rights to be free from prejudice and discrimination?

Prejudice

Prejudice specifically refers to making assumptions about people based on little evidence: pre-judging them. Often prejudice is based on common stereotypes, and it is likely to lead to discrimination.

Race Relations

"Race relations" refers to the relations between different ethnic groups within society and, as such, might be used when discussing race riots, for example. It is quite an old-fashioned phrase but leant its name to anti-discriminatory legislation passed in the 1970s and amended in 2000 and has therefore remained in the language even though modern legislation is more about issues of prejudice and discrimination in general rather than "race relations".

Racism

Racism is a form of *discrimination* on the basis of race, ethnicity, skin colour and related issues.

Rights

See the *Liberalism* chapter and glossary for a clear explanation of this liberal concept.

Sexism

Sexism is a form of *discrimination* on the basis of gender. It usually refers specifically to discrimination against *women* in a patriarchal society.

Women's Movement

The women's movement is another term for the *feminist* movement: people fighting for the rights and in the interests of women

EDUCATION

A. Key issues

Education in Britain is an area of great political controversy. Educationalists from differing ideological backgrounds have radically conflicting views about what education is for, how it should be organised, who should get it and how it should be paid for.

DISCUSSION: WHAT *IS* EDUCATION FOR?

In your group, have an open discussion about the *purpose* or *functions* of education. Should education be simply for the sake of learning (i.e. its own sake)? Should it be to meet the economic needs of society? Should it be to ensure everybody ends up in a suitable social role related to their skills and ability? Is it to ensure we have a knowledgeable population who can question and evaluate and therefore be at the forefront of progress? Do you have other thoughts about what education might be for?

Remember to consider formal and informal education, and education at all levels.

Whatever the functions of education, it clearly has a huge impact on people's life chances. Leaving formal education with an impressive set of qualifications opens doors to opportunities in society (and with that, money!) As education does have a clear impact on success and wealth, there is inevitably political interest in *access* to education and the issue of *equality* in education. Does everybody have the same opportunity to access that success and wealth? And, if they do, does a meritocratic system of deciding who can access success and wealth justify inequality?

Let's break down those ideas a bit and analyse them. There are two *equality* concerns about education.

One: do we have equal opportunities?

1. Do all pupils have equal access to quality education, regardless of their social background and wealth?

2. Are tests and exams fair?

3. Is progress to further educational opportunities and top jobs based purely on how pupils have performed in these tests and exams or might background, class, "old school tie" and nepotism get in the way of meritocracy?

Two: if we could be satisfied that we have all of those things (and that might be an impossible "if") would an unequal society in which some have great wealth and others are very poor be acceptable and justifiable? If so, there is a heavy price to pay for not being very good at exams; and a heavy responsibility on teachers to ensure that their pupils don't fall behind!

Until relatively recently, it was Conservative Party policy to reintroduce selective grammar schools: the 11+ system. It was their contention that this system was meritocratic. The brightest children, regardless of wealth or background, would get an academic education and this was a gateway to good universities and top jobs. Other pupils would receive an appropriate education to equip them for other work in the job market.

VIDEO: ANDREW NEIL ON GRAMMAR SCHOOLS

New Right journalist, Andrew Neil makes a strong argument for grammar schools, suggesting that it is the absence of grammar schools that has brought back the dominance of public schoolboys at the top of Britain's political parties. He does skate over Ed Miliband's comprehensive education.

Follow the link to the video:

What do you make of Andrew Neil's argument?

Would Harold Wilson or Margaret Thatcher have failed to excel had they attended comprehensive schools?

There are two clear "left-wing" criticisms of this. The first is to question how meritocratic that system really was. It is regularly pointed out, by socialist educationalists, that despite the apparent meritocracy in the system, the grammar schools were overwhelmingly the preserve of the middle class. Secondary modern schools were even more overwhelmingly the preserve of working-class pupils, as the better-off middle-class pupils would normally have an option in the independent sector should they fail the 11+.

It is easy enough to understand the middle-class "flight" from state secondary modern education as it was often portrayed as a "second class" education and, if parents were in a financial position to make a choice, independent schools would seem an attractive alternative. But why were the grammar schools so overwhelmingly middle class? They were not exclusively so, by any means. There were plenty of "grammar school boys" and girls who found themselves upwardly-mobile in terms of social class, through the grammar school system. (It ought to be borne in mind that there were "scholarship" boys and girls in the world before the 11+ who then, too, were able to access an academic secondary education from working-class backgrounds).

If we begin by dismissing that middle-class people might just generally be more intelligent (as that is clearly irrational!) there must be other explanations. A number have been suggested:

- *There is no true measure of intelligence.* The test at eleven was meant to decide who had an "academic" intelligence, who had a "technical" intelligence and who had a "practical" intelligence and, from that, determine which school they should attend. This was always viewed by pupils and parents as being more a test to decide whether people were intelligent or not. "Academic intelligence" was always seen as superior to the others. But what test could really measure this? For many years, the 11+ consisted of a maths test, an essay (or other piece of extended writing) and verbal and non-verbal reasoning tests. Success in the maths and writing tests was not necessarily a measure of intelligence, but rather a measure of the quality of previous education (including home education). Therefore highly-educated parents were a clear advantage (and this was obviously more common among middle-class pupils than working-class pupils). There is a wide range of reasons why working-class pupils might fall behind their middle-class peers at primary school, ranging from space, time and resources at home, to labelling, subcultures and language codes at school (see a good Sociology textbook if you want more information!) There is also the question of *what* people were asked to write in the writing test. Critics of the 11+ point to tests where people were asked to write a letter thanking the owners of a farmhouse where they have spent the summer holidays. This clearly favoured those pupils who might have had those experiences. Verbal reasoning tests were supposed to be measures of intelligence, not knowledge, but sometimes those who set the tests made cultural assumptions about existing knowledge (see example below). Tests show that people can get better and better at verbal and non-verbal reasoning tests or IQ tests. They do not become more intelligent, of course, they just get better at passing the tests, through extensive coaching and practice. Therefore, pupils whose families have the means to pay for coaching and to access old test papers, etc. have a much better chance of passing. Although modern grammar school entrance exams tend to just have the verbal and non-verbal reasoning tests, these are still very clearly nothing like an objective measure of intelligence.

- *Grammar schools were seen as middle-class schools.* While many working-class parents would be very proud of their children for passing the 11+, others might be concerned for a number of reasons. Back in 1944, the norm was to leave secondary school at 14, whereas grammar school children tended to stay to at least 16 and probably beyond. Families that were counting on an extra income in a few years time could see success at 11 as a negative thing rather than a positive one. Furthermore, parents might assume that their children would not fit in at the grammar school; that they might be bullied because of where they lived, how they spoke or their lack of resources. Not only that, pupils themselves might have seen the grammar school as the "posh" school and not wanted to go there, preferring to stay with their friends.

EXEMPLAR 1950s 11+ VERBAL REASONING QUESTION:

Which is the odd one out?

ZOMRAT

HRBAMS

LENDAH

REFUD

The answer is REFUD. Do you know why?

*It is an **anagram** question. If you do the anagrams, they are: Mozart, Brahms, Handel and Freud. Would you have been able to find the odd one out when you were eleven? Is it a test of verbal reasoning or general knowledge? Why might middle-class pupils in the 1950s be more likely to be able to answer this question?*

As we have seen, one criticism of selective education was that it was not really meritocratic. The modern Conservative Party under David Cameron would appear to have acknowledged this, favouring a large expansion of the Academies programme (started under the previous Labour government) rather than introducing more grammar schools.

But there is a more problematic criticism from the left. This argument questions whether a truly meritocratic system would be fair, even if one could be found. Of course not everybody can have access to the same university courses or all jobs, regardless of ability, skills and aptitude, but should one function of education be to make society more equal rather than just to make inequality "fairer"? This *egalitarian* approach to education sees equality in education as needing to go further than just equal *opportunities*. There need to be more equal *outcomes*.

What does this mean in practice? Ironically, when Rab Butler introduced the Tripartite System in 1944 (grammar schools, secondary modern schools, and technical schools) the assertion was that the three types of "intelligence" the schools were meant to cater for were "equal but different", whereas Tony Crosland, one of the egalitarian Labour pioneers of comprehensive education wanted "a grammar school education for everybody". However, while the 1944 Education Act might have presented academic, technical and practical "intelligences" as "equal but different" that was clearly not the practical reality. An academic education opened doors to university and the professions, social mobility and comparative wealth, while many deemed to have "practical intelligence" found themselves in non-examination classes, leaving school with no qualifications and moving on to a poorly-paid manual job. Very few technical schools were ever built.

For people like Crosland, the academic knowledge that was imparted in the grammar schools should have been given to everybody. They doubted that people could be fairly or reasonably pigeon-holed as "academic", "technical" or "practical" and believed that education had value for everybody, regardless of the needs of the economy and the jobs that they might go on to after school. For socialist egalitarians this was important because people who had been encouraged to be critical, evaluative, imaginative and creative at school, and introduced to great literature and great ideas, would not tolerate a society in which they were expected to graft for little reward with little or no prospect of change. For these people, society should be as equal as possible and inequality – whether based on apparently meritocratic principles, or on nepotism or aristocracy – was wrong.

However, in the 1970s, there was a growing argument (famously articulated by James Callaghan in his Ruskin College speech) that this "grammar school education for everybody" approach was not providing the British economy with the skills it needed. The economy did not require lots of people who had read Shakespeare (some of whom had understood it rather better than others), it needed engineers, or plasterers, or welders. It needed people with specific skills, and the education system was not fulfilling this need. Callaghan argued for a huge expansion in *vocational* education.

Many governments over the years have taken an interest in vocational education, traditionally at further education level, with GNVQs, BTECs, etc. but increasingly at younger ages. The last Labour government introduced the "diploma" system where pupils could follow a vocational pathway from the age of 14, doing a combination of school, college and workplace learning. At the same time there was a massive increase in the number of BTECs and vocational GCSEs offered in schools, in place of traditional GCSEs. Critics have suggested that this has essentially reintroduced selection and also that schools have used the comparatively easy vocational Level 2 courses to meet *targets* at the expense of educational *standards*. In other words, a distinction in some BTECs can be considered "equivalent" to four GCSEs at A*; however such a concentration in one subject area cannot really be considered as an equivalent, especially when it is likely to have been achieved entirely through centre-assessed coursework.

The promotion of the English Baccalaureate by Michael Gove and the current coalition government has been seen as an attempt to combat this latter trend. This apparent conflict between *targets* and *standards* is another key issue in education policy. Governments have been keen to set targets for schools and colleges and (overall) they have tended to meet them. Exam results have kept getting better year on year; A* grades have had to be introduced to differentiate at the top, to show that things have kept on getting better!

And yet, some argue that educational *standards* are slipping; that general levels of literacy and numeracy, etc. have fallen. This inevitably leads to discussions about whether exams have been "dumbed down". Every August, when A Level and GCSE results are published, there are two main themes to newspaper comment. There are articles praising the best results yet. And then there are articles saying the exams have become easier. Occasionally, a low-mark question from a GCSE foundation paper will be put in a newspaper column as apparent evidence of "dumbing down". There are further comments criticising certain subjects. People will express incredulity that Media Studies or Film Studies can really be considered an A Level. Of course, it would be good to see those same columnists attempt the exams they criticise to see how they would fare, but the arguments and debates do not go away.

Another key issue in education policy today is the issue of *funding*. How is education funded? This is an issue at all levels but has become a particularly hot political potato in relation to *higher education*.

In 1979, all university students got a full grant. It was not means-tested in any way. Of course, there were no tuition fees at all! The cost of tuition, along with the cost of maintenance, was paid for through general taxation. In the long summer holidays, students were able to claim unemployment benefit and housing benefit if they did not find a summer job. There was no such thing as student debt.

The end of summer benefits came quickly, followed by the steady introduction of means testing for grants. It was Conservative Education Secretary Ken Clarke who began gradually replacing the means-tested grant with a means-tested loan. Restoring full grants had been part of Labour Party policy for so long, that not everybody had noticed the change before 1997, when a Labour government was elected which got rid of grants entirely and introduced income-contingent loans instead. At least this was in their manifesto! A much bigger surprise came with the introduction of an up-front tuition fee, of £1000 a year. Students who were unable to pay the fees upfront were able to take out a loan to cover it. Significant levels of student debt had begun.

In the 2001 Labour Party manifesto, the party promised that it opposed "top-up fees" and had "legislated to prevent them". These were much higher university fees, favoured by many university vice chancellors, particularly in the Russell Group of universities, intended to effectively introduce a market in university education. The Russell Group's case was that levels of government funding for higher education were inadequate if they were to maintain quality. By the 2005 election, in direct contradiction of their 2001 commitment, the Labour government had legislated to introduce top-up fees of £3000 a year. To sweeten the pill, means-tested grants were restored.

The 2005 General Election was an interesting one because the Conservative Party promised to cut tuition fees entirely, and this did gain them some student votes, although there were concerns that they planned to significantly cap places. When the apparently right-wing Michael Howard was replaced with the apparently more moderate David Cameron, opposition to tuition fees was abandoned as a policy. They came into power in 2010 promising to maintain fees and to follow the advice of the Brown Report into university funding.

When that report arrived, so too did the new Conservative Party policy: fees of up to £9000 a year.

While Conservative policy had been changeable on this matter, the one party that had been consistently opposed to tuition fees was the Liberal Democrat Party, earning them considerable support in student areas. Just before the 2010 General Election, they amended their policy of complete abolition of fees. They announced that they would reduce fees incrementally, still aiming for an eventual abolition, but not rush it all at once because of the worrying global financial situation. In government they went along with the £9000 a year fees, despite all Liberal Democrat MPs signing a pledge to oppose any rises in fees. It was one of the key issues that contributed to the Liberal Democrats' devastating performance in the 2011 local elections.

The Labour Party found itself in a difficult position to make much political capital out of this situation, despite mass demonstrations and rioting. First, it was the Labour Party that introduced tuition fees in the first place; second, it was unclear what its alternative policy should be. At the 2010 General Election they, like the Conservatives, said they would wait for the Brown Report. In his leadership campaign, Ed Miliband argued for a "graduate tax" rather than the loans. However, the party is far from united on the issue, and there are general concerns about how a graduate tax would work and whether it would be preferable to loans and fees.

An important thing to remember in relation to the massive increase in tuition fees planned for 2012: this does not constitute an increase – even a modest one – in the funding of universities. The fee hike comes hand in hand with a massive cut in university teaching grants from government. Indeed, the government funding of arts and humanities subjects are being cut by 100% - the cost of teaching these courses will be met by student fees alone.

B. Key legislation and reform

The 1944 Education Act

The 1944 Education Act introduced free secondary school education for everybody and, as such, is often seen as being part of the raft of laws that made up the creation of the Welfare State in the 1940s. However, a key difference is that the Education Act was introduced by a Conservative-led wartime coalition government and by a Conservative education secretary: Rab Butler.

Although the 1944 Education Act introduced free secondary education for all, it did not envisage everybody attending the same schools. A central plank of the Act was the introduction of the Tripartite System.

GRAMMAR SCHOOL	This school was aimed at *academic* pupils (demonstrated through performance in the 11+ test). These schools would provide an academic education, like that provided in grammar schools and public schools prior to the 1944 Act. Pupils from these schools would be likely to go on to study A Levels, and perhaps continue in education and work in the professions.
TECHNICAL SCHOOL	This school was aimed at pupils considered to have *technical intelligence* – skills and aptitude that would be of particular value in technical occupations. This aptitude would again be demonstrated through the 11+ test. These schools would seek to equip pupils with the technical skills that would be required to work in many skilled occupations, and the schools would have technical resources to assist with this process. In actual fact, relatively few of these schools were built and in most parts of the country there was a two-tier system, rather than a tripartite system.
SECONDARY MODERN SCHOOL	The secondary modern school was presented as being for those with a "practical intelligence" but actually meant "everybody else". The vast majority of school pupils attended secondary modern schools when the tripartite system was the dominant system. Those who call for a return of grammar schools rarely mention these schools but they are, of course, two sides of the same coin. Of course, some secondary modern schools were excellent.

Criticisms of this system tended to focus on the idea that a test at the age of eleven could have such a major impact on somebody's future. Although the original legislation referred to the schools as being "equal but different", there was no escaping the perception that some *passed* (and went to the grammar school) while others *failed* and went to the secondary modern. Most pupils failed.

Comprehensive Education

Comprehensive education was not introduced by a single piece of legislation, nor is it associated with one party or secretary of state. Labour and Conservative governments introduced comprehensive schools to the UK and fewer and fewer areas kept the 11+ selective system.

One of the most enthusiastic reformers was Labour secretary of state for education, Tony Crosland. Crosland said that he wanted a "grammar school education for all" and, as such, his vision of a comprehensive school was primarily an *academic* one, although essentially what he meant by this was that everybody should get an equally *good* education. (One of the defences of grammar schools was that they tended to be good schools).

Crosland angrily promised to "close every f***ing grammar school in the country" if it was the last thing he did. In that respect, he failed, although the dominant system of secondary education certainly changed under Crosland.

In fact, it was a Conservative secretary of state, one Margaret Hilda Thatcher, who closed down the most grammar schools. For a long time, since the 1980s, it was a key policy of the Thatcherite tendency in the Conservative Party to have a grammar school in every town; many towns lost their grammar schools to Mrs. Thatcher's axe in the first place.

Critics of comprehensive schools felt that they did not stretch the brightest and also failed the weakest, by keeping them in classes they had no interest in and would get no value from. It was argued that the only way to get around this was to *stream* or *set* the pupils by ability, which still marked pupils out as "failures". These criticisms suggested that the schools failed the "meritocratic" test – the best pupils did not reach the heights they might have done at grammar school – and failed the "egalitarian" test – the weakest pupils were still failed by the system. However, supporters of comprehensive education would point to bright comprehensive pupils achieving outstanding results and would argue that it was the elitism at top universities and top professions that held back comprehensive pupils, not their comprehensive education itself. They would further point to the decrease in pupils leaving school without qualifications.

Some would argue that one of the problems with comprehensive schools is the vast inequalities *between* the schools, depending on their catchment area and competition from neighbouring schools. From this perspective there is a "postcode lottery" as to whether pupils get a good education in the comprehensive system. They would point to the fact that middle-class parents have learnt how to "play the system" and get pupils into the "best" comprehensive schools, meaning that the *social* inequalities that prevailed in the tripartite system were not fully eradicated by comprehensivisation.

However, there was no major Education Reform Act changing the structures of secondary education in the UK as a whole until 1988. The 1988 Act, brought in by secretary of state Kenneth Baker, was a radical reform by a New Right government.

The 1988 Education Reform Act

The 1988 Act brought in a number of key reforms which, as a package, could be seen as the *marketisation* of secondary education.

The Act brought in:

- *The National Curriculum* – much greater central control of what was taught and when; pupils in different schools and in different parts of the country to learn the same things at the same time

- *SAT Tests* – tests were introduced at 7, 11 and 14 (together with GCSEs at 16) that would measure pupils' attainment in relation to the National Curriculum

- *League Tables* – lists of schools would be published, showing their relative positions in terms of the results of the aforementioned tests

- *Schools funded "per head"* – funding for schools would be based on the number of pupils they had, therefore full schools would be well-funded (and would push for expansion) while less popular schools would get less funding

- *More choice of secondary school for parents* - parents were given more choice over which state secondary school they wanted their child to attend

- *Local management of schools* – Head teachers were given more control over their budgets, as opposed to education authorities

The Act also introduced GCSEs, OFSTED and compulsory staff training days (still known as "Baker days" in some schools). One of the main impacts of the Act was to remove powers and responsibilities from local education authorities and place them partly with the schools (the head teachers and governing bodies) and partly with central government (e.g. setting the curriculum and OFSTED).

There were all sorts of educational and strategic reasons for many of these policies, but in this module you are likely to be asked about the *ideological* case for these changes. As previously mentioned, this came from a New Right government – what were they hoping to achieve?

Marketisation. One clear intention of the 1988 Education Act was to introduce a market in education. By attaching money to pupils, making it easier for pupils to move between schools and easier to compare performance between schools (through the National Curriculum) and giving parents information about the relative position of schools on the league tables, a market was introduced. Because schools inevitably had a limited number of places, it was never a free market, but the intention was that successful schools would be rewarded, and unpopular schools would have a choice – to improve or die. There was a clear *incentive* to improve – if they could move up the league tables they could attract more parents, and with them, more funds. However, there was not necessarily a clear *ability* to improve, especially if their budgets were cut! The system did not take into account individual reasons why some schools might be lower down the league tables than others. (It was much later that "value added" league tables were introduced, which showed how well the school did with the pupils it had).

Control Some have argued that the 1988 Education Act also sought to take power away from local authorities and teachers, who the Conservative government considered to be too "liberal", left wing and occasionally "extremist". Of course, the neo-liberal element of New Right politics would want to see power taken away from the state, but the neo-conservative element would want to be sure that children were taught the *right* things at school.

It has been argued, then, that setting a National Curriculum and national tests and introducing a centralised regulatory body, rather than local inspectors, was as much about *control* as it was about establishing an education market. It was feared that left-wing Labour councils in places like London, Liverpool and Sheffield might have some strange ideas about what young people should be learning! This could be placed in the same context as the Thatcher government's decision to introduce "Section 28" that sought to restrict what could be taught about sexual orientation in schools. Schools were also given the option (and incentive) to "opt out" of local authority control and receive a direct grant from central government. Although this was criticised by the Labour opposition at the time, it had much in common with the "Academies" idea that Tony Blair was eventually to champion as Prime Minister.

Moving Beyond the "Bog-Standard" Comprehensive

The phrase "bog-standard comprehensive" came from an unlikely source, Alistair Campbell. Campbell has always been a great champion of comprehensive education. However, as press spokesman for Tony Blair, he was trying to sell New Labour education reforms that sought to introduce much more *diversity* in schools. While Crosland had wanted "a grammar school education for everybody" and much pro-comprehensive discussion had centred around making "every school a good school", the Blair government saw *educational diversity* and *parental choice* as key. There were a number of ways in which they sought to achieve this:

- More faith schools (controversial with some Labour activists who thought state education should all be secular)

- Academies (schools independent of local authorities which could access private funding)

- Specialist Schools (the issue Campbell was particularly referring to – encouraging schools to have a *specialism* and then for schools to collaborate)

Following these reforms various schools announced that they were "specialist sports schools", "specialist performing arts schools", "specialist engineering schools", "specialist language schools", etc. The specialisms, alongside a commitment to collaboration, gave the schools access to specialist funding streams. As such, specialist language schools got new language labs, performing arts school new drama studios, etc.

The idea was that parents could choose a local school partly based on that school's specialism and whether it tied in with their child's interests and strengths. Furthermore, language specialist schools could "lead" languages at a number of local schools who, in turn, could lead the way with their specialisms. Some of this happened in large towns and cities where schools with varied specialisms were located within a short distance of one another. In rural areas, it was quite unrealistic to imagine that the pupils at one school would gain any benefit from the excellent science resources at a "neighbouring" school perhaps ten or more miles away.

```
DISCUSSION: SPECIALIST SCHOOLS

Does / did your school have a "specialism"?  What was it?  How did
that specialism present itself in the day-to-day life of the school?  Did
pupils from other schools benefit from the specialism (as far as you
know)?  Did you benefit from the specialist resources of a
neighbouring school?


It is likely, if members of your groups went to a variety of schools, that
there will be some diversity of responses in your group.
```

Other New Labour Education Reforms

The Labour government also introduced some key reforms at both primary and
higher education level. At primary level, the government first focused on reducing
class sizes. Under the previous government, class sizes of over 30 were quite
regular; the Labour government put 30 as a cap for classes of pupil aged seven or
under. Also at primary level, the government decided to put a much a greater
emphasis on the key skills of *literary* and *numeracy*. To this end, they introduced
"literacy hour" and "numeracy hour" in the primary school curriculum. These were
really quite proscriptive, centrally-planned sessions designed to improve the number
of pupils leaving primary school with acceptable levels of literacy and numeracy
(partly responding to concerns about *educational standards*). How the sessions were
taught became gradually less proscriptive following concerns from teachers.

In higher education, the Labour government set a target of getting 50% of school
leavers to attend university. This target was in line with the sorts of numbers of
people going into higher education in many of the UK's "competitors", but was
criticised by some for potentially devaluing or "dumbing down" higher education.
At the same time as setting this challenging target, and having a clear aspiration to
widen participation in higher education, the government introduced tuition fees, as
previously mentioned. Although the aspirations of increasing university
recruitment and widening participation were inevitably put at risk by making
university education more expensive for the students, there is evidence to suggest
that the government was quite successful with both aspirations, although the
numbers of students quitting university during their course also increased.

There are a number of key aspects of the new government's education policy. We have already referred to the Higher Education policies, especially the new loans of up to £9000 a year. In schools, education secretary Michael Gove has focused on expanding Academies and introducing his controversial "free schools".

Under Labour, Academies were primarily intended to replace failing or failed schools in challenging areas. Controversial with people on the left of the party, the schools allowed companies, groups and wealthy individuals to help fund schools (with government assistance) that would be independent of local authority control. The system worked, in terms of failing schools turning around their fortunes, because it injected much-needed new funds as well as, often, bringing in new leadership.

When the Conservative Party abandoned its policy of having a grammar school in every town, its replacement policy was a massive expansion of Labour's Academies scheme. Instead of focussing on the schools that were struggling or in difficult inner-city areas, Gove saw Academy status as a *reward* for success for the best schools. As such, selective grammar schools were among those schools lining up to find new sources of funding under the new government. Even private schools investigated the possibility of becoming academies or "free schools". During the recession, some private schools found it harder to recruit because parents struggled to find school fees. Although getting academy status would mean the schools would have to stop charging fees, the injection of public money was certainly a tempting alternative. There was an interesting debate about whether schools could simply choose to return to private, fee-charging status once the economy recovered.

Gove's related idea was for new schools to be built where there was local demand. These schools were known as "free schools", based on the experience of similar schools in Sweden.

ARTICLE: FREE SCHOOLS FOR THE UK?

(First published on Suite101 in 2010 – see link for full article)

In 1993, the Swedish education system was "liberalised" to allow any group to set up a state-funded school. Since then, the 'free schools' or independent schools have grown: 10% of Swedish children now attend one. One argument in favour of this move was the idea that parents in rural areas, without access to a local school, could come together and receive funding for a school for their children. However, 70% of 'free schools' are located in the three main Swedish urban centres. The Conservative Party education spokesperson, Michael Gove, has often cited the Swedish free school system as the best model for future reform in the UK education system [1].

One problem for the Conservative Party, introducing this policy at a time when all parties are promising tight control of public spending, is that each new school costs money to establish, and some of the cost of this must come from the state. [2] The funding mechanism envisaged by Michael Gove and the Conservative Party is, like in Sweden, essentially a "voucher" system, where the money is attached to the pupil and therefore goes to whichever state school they choose to attend. The argument is that, in the long-run, this will be a more cost-effective approach to education. The popular schools will flourish and, in the fullness of time, unpopular, unsuccessful schools will be closed, saving waste.

But a 2004 report carried out by the Swedish National Agency for Education (or "Skolverket") discovered that 90% of the councils with free schools reported a significant increase in costs in order to set the schools up. The report also concluded that areas with a high proportion of free schools had a higher than average cost-per-pupil. This is after a decade of free schools. [3] The "Skolverket" report further suggests that "free schools" have not been the great success that Michael Gove and others have suggested. In Sweden, the proportion of fully-qualified teachers in the free schools is lower than in the "municipal" schools. Another central plank of Conservative education policy is to improve the overall qualifications of school-teachers.

The report also concludes that, of all the factors that might impact on innovation and quality in a school, whether it is "independently" or "municipally" run seems to be of little importance. 79% of local councils in Sweden also felt that competition with free schools had done nothing to drive up standards in the other schools in their area. There was also very little evidence of collaboration or partnership between schools.

Per Thulberg, the head of the National Agency for Education in Sweden, has stated categorically that following the Swedish system would not lead to improved educational standards. Indeed, in the "Trends in International Maths and Science Study" report of 2007, the UK was ranked higher than Sweden, and Swedish standards had fallen further than those of any other country. Although results are higher in the free schools, this – according to Thulberg – is because of social segregation. The pupils in the free schools come from wealthier backgrounds.

The 2004 study found that children in free schools had wealthier and more educated parents than those in the municipal schools. As well as segregation by social class, the agency has also reported an increase in segregation by academic performance and by ethnicity.

Sources:

[1] "Michael Gove: We Need a Swedish Education System." The Independent. 3 December 2008 [2] "The Conservative Party Education Manifesto," 2010. [3] "Schools Like Any Other? Independent Schools as Part of the System, 1991-2004." Skolverket, Swedish National Agency for Ed

122

Education Secretary, Michael Gove. 2010-?

C. Education and contemporary party politics

ACTIVITY: UP-TO-DATE POLICIES

Go to the websites of each of the three main political parties (there are clear links on the A2 Ideologies accompanying website). For each party, find their key, current policies relating to education. Most of these will be in a unique *education* section, although there might also be sections on *young people*, *skills* and *training* that are also relevant..

For each party, analyse their *current* policies about education in terms of the underlying *ideologies*

Keep this in your party policy file.

D. Answering exam questions on Education

Topic 2	**Education**
02	Explain the ideological case for SAT testing (10 marks)

SAT testing was brought in by the New Right conservative, Thatcher government, as one part of a wide range of reforms in the 1988 Education Reform Act

SAT testing was introduced alongside the National Curriculum and the publication of school league tables as well as reforms to how schools were funded and how places were allocated, all designed to create more of a *market* in education. The New Right ideology sees markets as being the best mechanism for effective and efficient decision-making.

By having a standardised test across the whole country, that tested all children on the same topics, and to then have those results published in the form of school league tables, arguably gave parents the information needed to participate in an education *market*.

New Right educationalists saw the advantage of *competition* both between schools (in trying to get higher up the league tables) and between pupils (in trying to get the best SATS results). New Right educationalists see regular testing, alongside other traditional educational methods, as being the best way to educate young people.

Critics say that children are now "over-tested" and that the SATS and league tables do not give a fair reflection of school performance.

```
┌─────────────────────────────────────────────────────────────────┐
│  Topic 2              Education                                   │
│                                                                   │
│                                                                   │
│  02      Explain the concept of meritocracy (10 marks)            │
│                                                                   │
│                                                                   │
└─────────────────────────────────────────────────────────────────┘
```

To answer this question, you would essentially define the concept, as in the glossary entry for *meritocracy* below. However, to get ten marks you would need to go some way beyond a general *description* of the term and, particularly, you will need to contextualise it in terms of ideologies about education.

A good way to do this would be to include a discussion about grammar schools. You can relate this to Andrew Neil's passionate support for grammar schools and his claim that the old grammar school system was more *meritocratic* than today's system, and that was why politicians from relatively modest backgrounds (like Harold Wilson or Margaret Thatcher) could reach the top, whereas now public-schoolboys, like Tony Blair or David Cameron, are the ones who get to the top. You could point out that it is often people on the political right (the neoliberal, New Right) who argue for this sort of *equality of opportunity* and raise some questions about it from both a social liberal and a socialist perspective. Can schools be truly and fairly meritocratic? Is meritocratic inequality justifiable, or – because it is unequal – is it still *bad*?

Have a go at this question and show it to your teacher!

The Thirty-Mark Question (6)

```
┌─────────────────────────────────────────────────────────────────┐
│  Topic 2              Education                                   │
│                                                                   │
│                                                                   │
│  02      "The educational policies of contemporary UK parties     │
│          are deeply                                               │
│          ideological." Discuss  (30 marks)                        │
│                                                                   │
│                                                                   │
└─────────────────────────────────────────────────────────────────┘
```

Have a go at this question, and then turn to the back of the book and compare with the model answer-plan.

E. Education Glossary

Competition

Competition, in relation to education, can refer to competition *within* the school (competitive sports, or children competing for their place in the class or for prizes) and competition between schools (schools competing for their place in the league tables, for parents to send their children to them and for funding). Conservatives have tended to favour competition – both within and between schools – while socialists have been less comfortable with this.

Comprehensive Schools

Comprehensive Schools are those state-funded schools where the children who attend them have *not* been selected on the basis of ability: children of all abilities are learning together under the same roof. They were introduced by Labour and Conservative governments from the 1960s onwards. They were most associated with Labour Education Secretary Tony Crosland, although Conservative Education Secretary Margaret Thatcher closed more *grammar schools* than any other Education Secretary.

Curriculum

Curriculum refers to what is taught in the schools. This might be a *national curriculum* (one curriculum, set by central government, that all schools have to follow) or be set by the school or the teachers (or exam boards). Some also talk about a "hidden curriculum" – all those things that are taught in schools without being part of the formal curriculum (e.g. obedience, hierarchy, time-keeping, respect for authority, etc.)

Education

Education is a difficult word to define! It is actually a *very* general word relating to all the ways in which learning takes place – not just formal education in terms of schools, colleges and universities.

Egalitarianism

Educationalists of the left have tended to take an egalitarian approach to education, rather than a meritocratic one. This approach is interested in equality of *outcome* not just equality of opportunity. Tony Benn talks about "the genius inside every child". The egalitarian view prefers comprehensive education with minimal setting and streaming, and is strongly opposed to selection.

League Tables

League Tables were introduced as part of the Conservative Education Reform Act of 1988. They were part of a general attempt to *marketise* education. They placed schools in order of children's attainment in standardised tests and made this information public to parents. They were criticised by teachers who felt that the tables by attainment were crude measures of a school's worth, leading to the later creation of "value added" league tables (showing how well pupils did at a school, taking into account the educational levels of the pupils on arrival at the school).

Meritocracy

A meritocracy is a society where people get where they are through their *merit* rather than through privilege, wealth or birth. A meritocracy is not an equal or egalitarian society; it is an unequal society but – its proponents would claim – a fair society because ability and hard work have determined where people end up. Left-wing critics (especially Marxists) would argue that meritocracy is a myth: privilege, wealth and birth do get people to their positions in society (look at David Cameron!) because their privilege helps them to be the winners in the apparently meritocratic systems.

Progressive teaching methods

Some "left-wing" teachers and educationalists were critical of traditional teaching methods – particularly learning by rote, a great emphasis on "the three Rs" and children being scared of their teachers. They introduced alternative approaches, learning through experience and activity, an emphasis on creativity and pupils' own experiences and more equal relationships. There were some extreme experiments with schools having few if any rules, etc. Some "right-wing" educationalists argue that progressive teaching methods are to blame for many of society's ills and for falling standards.

Selection

The 1944 Education Act introduced state secondary education for all, but based on a strictly *selective* system, where which school you could attend depended on how you performed in a test. In some parts of the country, this approach is still used for entrance to *grammar schools*. An extension of selection was Conservative Party policy until a recent change under David Cameron.

Standards

It is often said (particularly by educationalists on the political right) that educational *standards* are falling, despite exam results apparently always increasing. The argument is that people's standard of literacy and numeracy is lower than it has been in the past, even though people may be able to pass tests and governments meet their targets. A key part of this argument is the idea that exams have been "dumbed down".

Targets

Educational *targets* are set by government and might include a certain percentage of pupils getting 5 A*-C in their GCSEs, for example. There has been criticism of "target culture" in government overall; in terms of education, it might mean that targets are met *at the expense* of *standards*: i.e. people are trained to pass the tests or the exams, or are entered for relatively easy tests or exams to ensure the targets are met, rather than being stretched, pushed and encouraged to achieve their full potential.

Setting and Streaming

Setting refers to putting pupils into a group based on their ability for a specific subject (e.g. somebody might be in a set one for English and set four for Maths). Streaming is selection by ability within a school – pupils might be in an "A" stream or a "C" stream for all their classes.

Traditional teaching methods

Right-wing educationalists favour *traditional* teaching methods as opposed to *progressive* ones. They would point to apparently falling *standards* as evidence that traditional teaching methods were superior. As such they would favour learning by rote, "chalk and talk", and very strong discipline. Some might favour a return to *corporal punishment*.

Vocational Education

Vocational Education is all education that is specifically aimed at preparing pupils / students for a specific job, rather than for their general or academic development. Particularly associated with Further Education colleges, but increasingly part of school curricula too, vocational qualifications have been regularly reformed over the years, leading to a great number of competing qualifications (BTECs, NVQs, Vocational A Levels, Applied A Levels, HNC/Ds, etc)

ECONOMY

A. Key issues

Perhaps the biggest issue relating to the economy in modern politics is the question of the role of the state. Indeed, this question is at the heart of much ideological difference. What role, if any, should government have in the economy?

For socialists, traditionally at any rate, there has always been a major, active role for the state. This can be seen in terms of *economic planning* and *public ownership*. Since the Second World War, this can also be seen in terms of *macroeconomics*.

Economic Planning – Traditionally, socialists have seen economic planning as a legitimate role for the state. Governments can look at the economy as a whole and plan what should happen and when. Famous, if extreme, examples would be Stalin's five year plans in the Soviet Union, that saw the country rapidly industrialise in a relatively short period of time. In Britain, Labour governments have set about planning the future development of the economy, such as Wilson's decision to transform the UK into a centre of technology (put forward in his "white heat of technology" speech).

Traditionally, economic liberals and modern conservatives have preferred to leave such things to the free market: a laissez-faire approach. It is industrialists and capitalists, through the workings of the market, who can best shape and develop the future of the economy, they would argue. However, the current Conservative-led coalition government have talked about "rebalancing" the British economy in favour of manufacturing, which could be seen as an economic plan, even if the tools it intends to use to achieve this are those of the market and removing red tape and regulation.

Public Ownership – Also key to socialism, traditionally at least, was the concept of public ownership. For early socialists, much of this was in terms of *municipal ownership*, i.e. local government owning services and utilities. There was always an aspiration, however, for national ownership of industry: *nationalisation*.

For most socialists, nationalisation was about a combination of *democratisation* and *economic planning*. If industries and services were owned by the state, then any economic plan could be more easily and directly administered. But more importantly, if an industry were owned by a democratic government, then it would be subject to democratic pressures: without those pressures the bosses were the unaccountable dictators of their workers.

In fact, when a Labour government came to introduce a number of nationalisations, in the 1945-51 government, it was the *planning* aspect of nationalisation that was to the fore, and Herbert Morrison developed a peculiar form of nationalisation (sometimes called Morrisonian nationalisation) where the boards of the nationalised industry were largely autonomous from government, able to operate as a top-down organisation not so very different from how a private company might operate. Disappointment with Morrisonian nationalisation contributed to many democratic socialists in the 1970s and 1980s investigating *industrial democracy* (finding ways for bosses and managers to be genuinely accountable to their workers).

Although we often talk about a period of post-war consensus between Labour and the Conservatives, the Conservative Party consistently opposed nationalisations. It was not until the 1980s that Conservative governments set about *privatising* the utilities and other industries and services nationalised by the Labour governments.

Following the Thatcher and Major governments, that privatised the vast majority of state assets (including, most controversially, the railways under Major) the Labour governments of Blair and Brown appeared to have been converted to private ownership, not seeking to renationalise anything and indeed having a few of their own privatisations.

It is in the area of *macroeconomics* that most controversy in economic policy has been fought out in the 20th century. It is still controversial today, in a world beset by economic crisis.

Before the contribution of John Maynard Keynes, governments – left or right – did not really believe they were able to have much impact on the very big economic picture, on growth or recession; on boom or bust. Keynes put forward the argument that *fiscal policy* (tax and spend) could be used to boost or cool the economy as a whole: a *macroeconomic* policy as opposed to a *microeconomic* one. Before Keynes, governments increased taxation because they needed more revenue, and they spent money because a new project cost money, or a particular service required investment. These were *microeconomic* decisions. Keynes showed how government decisions over taxation and spending could take money out of – or put money into – the economy, thus promoting growth, alleviating the effects of recession, or indeed cooling down an excessive boom.

Raising taxes could, therefore, take money out of the economy. This has the effect of *cooling* the economy. This might be necessary if there appears to be an unsustainable boom. The government is also able to put money *into* the economy, both through tax cuts and through spending. If spent wisely, this money does not just help the specific focus of the investment, it has "multiplier effects" that benefit the whole economy. Keynes was able to point to the true cause of economic growth immediately prior to the Second World War in the UK and the USA: rearmament. Government spending on arms and munitions had a knock-on effect on the rest of the economy: investment with a specific microeconomic purpose kick-started the economy as a whole. Munitions factories needed raw materials and components, both the munitions plants and the providers of materials and components created employment. Employed people spend more money, boosting shops and commerce. For Keynes, the key aim of government economic policy should always be high rates of employment (preferably full employment).

Keynes' arguments were not universally popular. Economic liberals were not keen on taxation or public spending, for macro or micro economic reasons! American neo-liberal economist Milton Friedman (a great influence on Margaret Thatcher and other New Right figures) developed a neo-liberal macroeconomic alternative to *Keynesianism*: *Monetarism*.

For Friedman, Keynesian macroeconomics required far too much intervention in the economy on the part of the state. Fiscal policy should always, from his perspective, be low tax and low spend. However, he did see a macroeconomic role for the state in terms of *monetary* policy: interest rates. He did not see this in terms of managing growth and recession – this was an *economic cycle* over which government could have very little influence. Instead he saw the focus of government to be managing *inflation*. Indeed, some monetarists would argue that full employment was not even desirable: some unemployment ensured competition in the employment market preventing wage inflation. (This argument has led some on the left to accuse neo-liberal governments of managing "structural unemployment", i.e. deliberately keeping people unemployed).

Central banks (e.g. the Bank of England in the UK) set the base interest rates; the various rates of interest set by banks on their accounts and loans directly relate to this base rate. Whether interest rates are high or low has one major impact: whether people are likely to borrow money or save it. If interest rates are low, people (and companies) are likely to borrow money, and they borrow money in order to *spend* it. However, if everybody is spending too much and too freely, this can be *inflationary* as high demand encourages increased prices. When inflation increases, Friedman argues that interest rates should be raised, encouraging people to save rather than borrow, slowing down demand and therefore slowing down the inflationary pressure on prices.

Friedman's neo-liberal ideology led him to favour monetary policy to be administered *independently* of political control, preferably by computer. His view was that a computer could simply adjust the interest rate in light of the inflation rate.

Because Britain has a high level of home ownership, low interest rates tend to be popular. Hence, when governments have control of monetary policy there is a tendency to use it for electoral ends rather than economic ones (just as there is with fiscal policy). Therefore, if an election is coming up, reduced taxation and reduced interest rates can be a vote-winner. The macroeconomic impact of the policies can be dealt with after the election! As such, the Labour government's decision, in 1997, to make the Bank of England independent has been viewed as bringing the management of monetary policy closer to that envisaged by Friedman. However, members of the monetary policy committee (MPC) at the Bank of England would argue that there cannot be a simple equation relating inflation rates to interest rates. In the UK in 2011, inflation was far above the Bank of England's target; this should (on Friedman's analysis) have triggered an increase in interest rates. However, the macroeconomic picture was one of a national economy stagnated, with little or no evidence of growth. Discouraging borrowing and encouraging saving in such a situation, though it might have the desired effect on inflation, might threaten growth and cause the dreaded "double-dip" recession. Furthermore, bankers pointed to the fact that some of the causes of high inflation were out of Britain's control. Increased interest rates would not bring down the price of oil, for example: these prices were affected by *international* pressures, not national ones. This introduces the very important question of *globalisation*.

Globalisation

Globalisation is not just an economic concept; it relates to political, social and cultural change as well. However, it is argued that in relation to the economy, globalisation has given national governments very little room to manoeuvre. Although politicians can do what they can to change the economic picture, global events, patterns, trends and decisions are what really drives the economy; there is not really any such thing as "the British economy" any more, it is just part of the global economy.

This has long been the case. Tony Benn often recounts an event, when he was Secretary of State for Industry, when Henry Ford Jr. came to see him with a direct threat: that the government did what Ford Motorcars wanted, or they would move their operations out of the UK, at the cost of thousands of jobs.

Clearly one important aspect of economic globalisation is the power of transnational corporations, and their ability to operate anywhere in the world. A government can set a minimum wage, for example, but transnational corporations can always find people to work for less; in fact by relocating to the poorest parts of the world, some transnational corporations have virtually got rid of labour costs altogether. This leads almost inevitably to a "global division of labour" where some jobs are only done in the sweatshops of the developing world, while the developed world focuses on service sector jobs and financial services.

Another result of this extraordinary level of interconnectedness is the extent to which economic crisis and catastrophe spreads across the world. Decisions taken in one place can have a devastating effect somewhere else. Huge crises seem to move around the planet, from country to country, with the Eurozone currently being the focus of major concerns.

WEB TASK: GLOBALISATION

Follow the *Globalisation* links from the website to see a number of short films about globalisation and its impact. *Hyperglobalists* think that globalisation is an overwhelmingly positive process, while *pessimistic globalists* see it as a largely negative one. What do you think? Give reasons for your conclusion.

B. Key developments

From the 1940s until the 1970s, the macroeconomic theories of John Maynard Keynes were very influential on governments, whether Labour or Conservative. For a long time this approach appeared to be very successful: people talk about "the long boom" after the Second World War.

However, in the 1970s, the UK economy went downhill very quickly. Criticisms of the *Keynesian consensus* came from left and right. On the left, there was concern that the UK had adopted "neo-corporatism", a modern version of the preferred economic policy of fascist parties in the 1930s. They worried that trade unions had been co-opted into the establishment and that government, the leaders of industry and right-wing union barons were able to set the agenda in their own interests, against the interests of the working class. From the right, the concern was the unions had become too powerful and could hold the country to ransom. There was further concern that government interference and union power stifled the dynamism of the market and prevented innovation and progress.

This led to a significant *polarisation* of politics in the late seventies and early eighties, where the Labour Party swung to the left and the Conservative Party swung to the right. Clearly it was the Conservative Party that won the struggle with Margaret Thatcher coming to power in 1979 and remaining Prime Minister for more than a decade.

Margaret Thatcher's economic policies were greatly influenced by Friedman and his monetarist ideas. She also set about restricting the powers of trade unions with a number of pieces of legislation, collectively known as the anti-union laws (by trade unionists!) Thatcher's government also privatised a large number of public assets, work continued by both the Major and (to a lesser extent) the Blair governments.

In fact, the change from Conservative governments to New Labour governments did not spell a significant change in economic policy. The introduction of a minimum wage was clearly a significant piece of government intervention in the economy, but most of the anti-union laws were left intact and private ownership continued to be preferred to public ownership. As previously mentioned, Gordon Brown's move to give the Bank of England independence owed much to the ideas of Milton Friedman. Brown cited Adam Smith as a significant influence; Mrs Thatcher was also a disciple.

It was only with the recession and banking crisis late in the period of Labour governments that the Conservative and Labour parties really demonstrated different philosophies in relation to the economy. Some would argue that the philosophical differences were still essentially rather slight (both parties promised cuts in public spending at the 2010 General Election, even though there were differences relating to *what* they wanted to cut and the *speed* of the proposed cuts). However, when the Labour government took an essentially Keynesian approach to the crisis, investing heavily in industry, infrastructure and training, the Conservative party preferred a *laissez-faire* approach, opposing most spending commitments.

As Chancellor, George Osborne has attempted to pursue an "austerity", low-spend agenda. However, the looming threat of "double-dip" recession has led some to ask if he has a plan B. In many ways, the danger of recession during stringent cuts supports Keynes' view, while the risk of high inflation during a period of low interest rates supports Friedman.

C. Contemporary party politics and Economics

ACTIVITY: UP-TO-DATE POLICIES

Go to the websites of each of the three main political parties (there
are clear links on the A2 Ideologies accompanying website). For
each party, find their key, current policies relating to the economy.
These might well be spread quite widely across their policy
documents. There might be a specific section on *The Economy*, but
look also at sections on *business, industry, manufacturing,
globalisation*, etc.

For each party, analyse their *current* policies about the economy in
terms of the underlying *ideologies*

Keep this in your party policy file.

D. Answering exam questions on the Economy

Topic 3	The Economy
01　Explain what is meant by the term 'macroeconomics' (10 marks)	

Most economic thinking, before the early 20th century, was focused on specific, narrow questions: what we might call *microeconomics*. John Maynard Keynes, a British liberal economist, was interested in the economy as a whole, and proposed an approach to economic policy that could manage the state of the whole national economy and where the country was on the "economic cycle" (something that had previously been considered out of the government's control). His particular approach to macroeconomics, known as Keynesianism, was based on how government's could use fiscal policy (i.e. taxation and spending) to promote growth or to cool the economy down. Raising or lowering taxation alongside increasing or cutting public spending could put money into the economy or take it out where appropriate.

The other key macroeconomic theory of the 20th century was *monetarism*, developed by neoliberal economist, Milton Friedman. Friedman's macroeconomic policy was developed as a challenge to Keynesianism. For Friedman, the only legitimate macroeconomic role for government was in terms of *monetary* policy (although he would have liked to have seen it done by a computer, rather than by officials). While Keynes' chief concern was unemployment, Friedman was most concerned about inflation, and explained how changes to the base rate of inflation could impact on inflation (high interest rates encouraged people to save rather than spend; low interest rates encouraged people to borrow and spend).

Both these contrasting macroeconomic approaches are hugely influential on modern governments and economic policy-makers.

Topic 3   **The Economy**

01   What is the difference between fiscal policy and monetary policy? (*10 marks*)

Government economic policy is often divided up between *fiscal policy* and *monetary* policy. Fiscal policy refers specifically to levels of taxation and public spending (and, directly relating to spending, public *borrowing*). When government departments come up with policies, most will include some spending commitments; these will need to fit into the Treasury's fiscal policy parameters. Since the work of John Maynard Keynes, governments see overall fiscal policy – levels of taxation and public spending – in terms of their impact on the overall economy. Governments are also likely to have targets, and possibly rules, over levels of public borrowing. Gordon Brown had his "iron laws" of fiscal responsibility that had to be abandoned in the banking crisis. The US government had to raise its federal debt ceiling in 2011 in order to be able to meet its spending commitments.

Monetary policy on the other hand, relates to the setting of interest rates, which – as noted by Milton Friedman – has a subsequent impact on rates of inflation. Gordon Brown famously gave away responsibility for monetary policy from the Treasury by making the Bank of England independent. While both fiscal and monetary policy have a macroeconomic impact, they refer to very different aspects of economic policy. Keynesians believe governments can use fiscal policy to stimulate and cool down the economy, managing growth and protecting employment. Monetarists believe governments can use monetary policy to promote saving or borrowing and therefore have an impact on overall rates of inflation.

The Thirty-Mark Question (7)

Topic 3	The Economy
02	"There are now no significant differences in economic policy between the main UK political parties." Discuss (*30 marks*)

Attempt this question and then turn to the model essay plan at the back of the book. What did you miss? Did you make any points that are not included in the plan? Use both to revise from.

E. Economy Glossary

Capitalism

Capitalism is the dominant economic system in the world today. It is a system based upon the accumulation of capital by capitalists. Capitalists are the owners and controllers of businesses and industries. Most people associate capitalism with free market economics (although left-wing critics of the Soviet Union accused it of "state capitalism"). Capitalism is a system where private companies and corporations operate in order to make profits.

Debt

Of course being in debt simply means that you have borrowed money and you still have to pay it back. Although politicians have tried to equate public debt with personal debt, in order to make political points, the two are rather different. If you have personal debt you need to minimise your spending, maximise your income and pay it off; if you are a government with public debt, you have to take into account the impact that your spending might have on your income. Spending cuts might have an unexpected impact on income (decreased tax revenues, for example) and indeed might lead to new increases in spending (welfare payments, for example).

Economic Cycle

People often talk about an "economic cycle", referring to the fact that economies seem to move inevitably form growth to recession – a cycle of "boom and bust". As such people talk about where a national economy is on the "economic cycle", therefore some growth suggests that the economy is heading in the right direction (unless there is the dreaded "double-dip recession").

The Euro

The Euro is the single currency of the European Union. It was policy under the Labour Government to join the Euro if the UK economy passed certain tests; this effectively gave Gordon Brown the Chancellor a veto over the UK joining the Euro.

Fiscal Policy

Fiscal Policy refers to government's taxing and spending. Traditionally taxation was used to raise much-needed funds that could then be spent on public services, etc. but Keynes added another element to fiscal policy: that taxation and spending could be used as macro-economic tools to put money into the economy, or take it out again.

Globalisation

Globalisation is not just an economic phenomenon. It is a word used to describe the idea that the world is becoming smaller in a wide range of ways: economically, politically, socially and culturally. Economic globalisation is apparent in that concepts like "the British economy" or "the US economy" are increasingly meaningless: they are all at the mercy of the global economy. Decisions taken in the UK could have a massive impact half the world away, and vice versa.

Inflation

Inflation is the rate at which prices are increasing in an economy. There is more than one measure of inflation, but whichever measure is used, the prices of a sample of goods are measured and the rate of inflation is based on how much more expensive they are now compared with a year ago. Therefore, if inflation is 5%, that means that (on average) products are 5% more expensive than they were this time last year. What products are included in the sample can have quite a marked impact on the rate. Monetarists see inflation as the key economic priority for governments and, as prices are affected by supply and demand, macroeconomic policy can keep inflation under control.

Keynesianism

The economic theory of John Maynard Keynes that used fiscal policy for macroeconomic ends: particularly the view that government spending could stimulate demand and therefore kickstart economic growth.

Monetarism

Monetarism is a macroeconomic alternative to Keynesianism that focuses on monetary policy rather than fiscal policy and is most associated with the economist, Milton Friedman. For Friedman, the biggest economic evil is not unemployment but *inflation*. Controlling the rate of inflation is, for Friedman, the only legitimate macro-economic role for government, and they are able to do this through changing interest rates. Friedman was such an instinctive neo-liberal that he preferred the idea of a *computer* responding to inflation rates and setting interest rates accordingly, rather than leaving it up to politicians.

Monetary Policy

Monetary policy relates specifically to the setting of interest rates. In Britain today, the Monetary Policy Committee is based in the Bank of England and decides when and whether to alter interest rates in the light of economic performance and forecasts (primarily in relation to the rate of *inflation*.)

Privatisation

Privatisation is the process of selling off publically-owned assets to the private market. Famous examples would include the privatisations of several key utilities by the Conservative government in the 1980s and 90s, e.g. British Telecom, British Rail, British Gas, etc. The reasons for privatisation might be to raise some public revenue quickly, but might also be for ideological reasons: the New Right, for example, oppose state interference in the market, and assume that private enterprise will always be more efficient than public "bureaucracy".

Public Borrowing

The government needs money to do everything that it does – to spend on health, education, welfare, the military, defence, etc. It acquires this money through a number of different means, one of which is *borrowing*. The government borrows money from the private markets and, as such, is generally in debt. At times, public debts can be very high indeed. Governments like to keep a lid on borrowing; Gordon Brown had an "iron rule" of borrowing (to keep it below a certain percentage of GDP) which had to be abandoned in the banking crisis.

Public Spending

Public spending is all the money that the government spends. It raises revenue through taxation, borrowing and possibly privatisation or realising assets in other ways, so that it can spend money.

Taxation

Taxation is one of the key ways in which governments raise revenue. Taxation can include income tax, corporation tax, purchase taxes (like VAT or duties on products like cigarettes or alcohol) or one-off taxes (like inheritance tax or a "windfall tax"). Income tax and corporation tax are *direct* taxes while VAT (for example) is an *indirect* tax.

Unemployment

Governments record the number of people who are out of work, and it is a measure of the state of the economy. Measures of unemployment might be everybody who is "economically inactive" or it might be those who are claiming Jobseekers Allowance. Various governments have been accused of manipulating the statistics over the years. Keynesians see dealing with unemployment as the economic priority of any government, while monetarists think inflation should be the priority.

THE ENVIRONMENT

A. Key issues

For much of the twentieth century, the environment was a fringe concern in British politics. That is not to say that it was a "non-issue"; some of the most passionate and well-organised pressure groups were environmental ones. Greenpeace of course springs to mind, but the RSPB has been one of the largest and most influential environmental pressure groups, at the forefront of several key changes in the law.

But it was when environmental problems went global that they started to reach the mainstream. Campaigns to protect rare birds were one thing, but campaigns to protect *the planet* were on a wholly different scale.

In the 1980s and 1990s a number of key environmental issues began to be discussed and, to a certain extent, addressed.

- *Acid Rain* – There was a major concern about the impact that pollution had on rain; this meant that pollution in the UK could cause the destruction of forests and habitats in Scandinavia: environmental politics went international

- *The Ozone Layer* – Scientists found a hole in the ozone layer above the Antarctic, allowing harmful rays from the sun into the Earth's atmosphere. They linked this with the presence of certain chemicals in aerosols. The idea that human behaviour was having a major impact on the planet and the atmosphere pushed environmental politics into the mainstream

- *The Greenhouse Effect* – Increasingly environmentalists talked about "greenhouse gases" – the product of human activity and industry – that were causing the planet to get warmer, with a whole host of terrifying potential consequences. Green politics became apocalyptic!

Since the 1990s it is the subject of *climate change* and specifically *global warming* and its association with carbon emissions that has become the key topic of environmental controversy in global politics. Some environmentalists have expressed concern that other environmental issues have been entirely sidelined by this preoccupation. For example, many have championed *nuclear energy* as a clean alternative to coal and oil, forgetting the environmental movement's long campaign against nuclear energy, based on concerns about radioactivity, security and disposing of nuclear waste. Because these are not *climate change* issues, it almost now seems like they are not *green* issues.

Even with the news full of environmental catastrophe, and young people and students embracing green politics in large numbers, mainstream politicians of left, right and centre, did little more than pay lip service to green concerns until 1989, when the Green Party performed very well in the European Parliament elections.

Suddenly, being green was not just trendy, or even "just" essential: it was a potential vote winner.

Is Green politics left wing or right wing?

Initially, the green agenda seemed to fit most neatly with the political left. This was not just true in the UK where Labour, in opposition, were clearly keen to use the environment as a stick to beat the Conservatives with; throughout Europe, growing Green parties chose to form coalitions with parties of the left (e.g. the Social Democrats in Germany). The Green Party in Britain is, and was, clearly a left-wing party, taking social democratic or socialist positions on most issues that do not directly relate to the environment.

There are a number of potential reasons for this. There had always been a fringe element in socialist movements who promoted environmental matters before the 1990s made it fashionable. Many policies that were proposed to help the environment required levels of *economic planning* and various interventions in the market. This was difficult to square with Thatcherite conservatism, and easier to fit into a social democratic or socialist perspective. Many environmental problems required *international* solutions and, again, the left had a greater tendency towards internationalism and international cooperation. Finally, many of the people who were attracted to environmental politics also happened to be attracted to social liberal, social democratic or socialist politics when it came to other issues. Environmentalism often went hand-in-hand with a broadly egalitarian, humanist view, sometimes including a pacifist perspective. These positions meant that environmentalists could find common cause with some Liberal Democrats and people on the centre and left of the Labour Party. It might also be added that more radical environmentalists and more radical socialists are united in their "anti-capitalism".

However, some environmentalists believed that economic liberalism – the free market – could be an agent of *conservation*. One of the great concerns of environmentalists, in the 1990s as now, was the issue of the exhaustion of scarce resources. Some environmentalists saw the *price mechanism* as a way of conserving these. As resources become scarce, they become *expensive* and that both dampens down demand and provides people with an incentive to find alternatives. As such, some environmentalists welcomed the Conservative privatisation of water, and especially the introduction of water meters, in the hope that such measures would lead people to be less wasteful. Other environmentalists saw the privatisation of water as theft of public property – so there was quite a broad range of environmental views here.

Finally, there is a whole tradition of environmentalists who refuse to be seen as left wing or right wing and are not prepared to be an "add-on" to somebody else's ideology. These "dark green" thinkers see ecologism as a distinct ideology that condemns both the politics of the left and the right. For these thinkers, all the mainstream ideologies are focused on economic *growth* (even if they come at it from very different angles and for very different ends). For them, growth is not a positive thing, it is a wholly negative thing that is destroying the planet and destroying eco-systems and habitats around the world. Human beings have to find a way to exist in the world in a balanced and natural way, and to do this they need to cast off the trappings of prosperity and growth and return to nature.

Although this is a very radical view, which can include arguments for banning cars and living in forests, there are strange and unlikely echoes of other ideologies. Early, traditional conservatism had its anti-industrialism which included a concept of a pre-industrial pastoral idyll or "golden age". Utopian socialists also often used a pre-capitalist, pre-industrial picture as the model for their image of the future. Fascists too were also often anti-industry and pastoral imagery was employed by them. Indeed there was some evidence of environmentalist positions and argument pursued by some fascists, especially in Nazi Germany. Believe it or not, there is such a thing as an "eco-fascist"!

Green thinking, then, is often described in terms of its *shade* of green: light or dark.
"Dark green" politics remained very much on the fringes of politics, but light green
ideas found their way into pretty much every manifesto and policy document that
any mainstream party published.

People now also talk about another shade of green thinking, neither light nor dark:
bright green thinking.

Bright green thinking is marked out by its optimism. Like *dark green* thinking, it
appreciates that light green solutions are not sufficient to save the planet – if we all
stopped leaving our TVs on standby and recycled all the rubbish we can, that is not
enough to reverse global trends. However, unlike *dark green* thinkers, people who
take a "bright" approach believe that science and technology *can* provide solutions
to the environmental crisis, providing that the political will is there and the
investment is provided. Bright green environmentalists do not turn their backs on
progress: it is through new technology, science and development that solutions can
be found. Some already have been: renewable energy sources, electric cars, carbon-
capture technology. Given sufficient resources and political will, scientists can
answer the challenging questions that climate change poses.

There has been something of a political backlash against environmentalism in recent years. Questions raised over some of the science of climate change have led to an increase in "climate change deniers" and conspiracy theories about hidden agendas behind green politics. Most of these doubts and questions have emerged from the *right* (although Cameron's conservatives seem largely immune from them). For some time the only scientists openly questioning global warming were those whose research was paid for by Exxon Mobil or Texaco, and politicians who expressed doubts were openly ridiculed. However, scepticism about whether global warming is a manmade phenomenon is a position that is growing quickly, and it will be interesting to see if such views make it into the political mainstream and, if they do, what impact they might have. This needs to be seen in the context of some "green" policies being very unpopular. Increased taxes on fuel and air travel, for example, will never be big vote winners.

B. The Environment and Contemporary Party and Pressure Group Politics

However, until 2005, the level of environmental concern in the parties could probably be ranked: Liberal Democrats (most concerned), Labour (second most) and Conservative (least). When David Cameron sought to rebrand the Conservative Party, one of the main features of that change of image was a change of priorities relating to the environment. He demonstrated this in a number of ways:

- *New Logo* The Conservative Party ditched the blue torch and replaced it with a green tree

- *Cycling to work* As the new Tory leader, David Cameron got a good deal of media attention for cycling to work each day, intending to set an example that others might follow. When his old friend Boris Johnson became Mayor of London, he too chose to cycle everywhere. Cameron's media performance was undermined somewhat by the revelation that a driver followed him with his suit and a change of shoes.

- *Press Conference from a Glacier* Still very early in the Cameron leadership, he chose to make a key statement on climate change from a shrinking Norwegian glacier. Again, this attracted some criticism as his journey there, for the brief media performance, was not the most environmentally-friendly trip going.

- *Zac Goldsmith* One of Cameron's friends was the high-profile environmental campaigners (and millionaire) Zac Goldsmith. Goldsmith's decision to join the Conservative Party and stand as a candidate for the party gave them a degree of green credibility.

The Labour Party and the more left-wing parts of the media argued that this was all a show and nothing more than a rebranding exercise. They argued that the Conservative Party needed something different to talk about rather than Europe or immigration in order to try and shake off their label of being "the nasty party". In making this accusation, they were saying that the Conservative Party were not even "light green" but instead "lite green". This is a charge levelled at organisations or companies that use green language in their marketing in order to get outcomes that have nothing to do with the environment (e.g. usually to make more money!)

Did Cameron's Conservatives mean it? It's probably too early to say for sure. It was noticeable that, as the 2010 general election loomed and economic issues took centre stage, the environment seemed to drop off the agenda. However, when it came to election manifestos themselves, all three mainstream parties put forward remarkably similar proposals on the environment. While most of these would be considered *light green* there was also some *bright green* thinking here too. All the parties talked about "the green economy" and investing in "green jobs". The parties no longer just talked about meeting their obligations from international treaties (like Kyoto and Copenhagen); they talked about leading the way. The optimistic, science and technology-driven agenda of *bright green* thinking appeared to have influenced all the parties. This was probably helped by the prospect of an *economic* benefit to investing in bright green innovation: this could create jobs and help to kickstart the ailing economy.

WEB TASK: ENVIRONMENTAL POLICY

Go back to the websites of all three main UK parties and find the section in their policy statements on the *environment*. How much importance or emphasis do they place on these policies? In what ways do the policies differ? I what ways are they the same?
Analyse them in terms of whether they represent *light green*, *dark green* or *bright green* thinking.

File with your other analyses of party policy.

The 2010 general election also saw the Green Party getting their first MP in Westminster. Caroline Lucas, the party's leader, sits in parliament and, although she does not follow any whip, she has tended to vote quite similarly to the left-wing MPs in the Labour Party, as one might expect, and has been strongly critical of the budget cuts agenda of the Conservative Party.

WEB TASK: THEY WORK FOR YOU

The "They Work for You" website summarises how MPs have voted on key issues as well as providing links to speeches they have made in Parliament, questions they have asked, etc. Follow the link from the A2 Ideologies website and analyse how Caroline Lucas has voted and what areas she seems to have focused on. Are her positions ideologically coherent? Justify your answer. Now do the same for environmentalist and Conservative MP, Zac Goldsmith.

The main focus of environmental politics is still in the world of extra-parliamentary activity and pressure groups. There are a wide range of groups including some insider groups that seek to make changes to environmental legislation primarily through consultation and negotiation with government and other agencies (e.g. the RSPB) and outsider groups, like Greenpeace. Greenpeace divides its attention between environmental issues and pacifist ones, with much of its direct action in recent years being focused on the wars in Iraq and Afghanistan. However, they have also been very active on environmental matters, such as the debate over a third runway at Heathrow.

CASE STUDY: THIRD RUNWAY AT HEATHROW

This is a good area on which to do some research. Try and identify the relative impact of pressure groups and parliamentarians on decisions over the third runway. Also try and analyse the relative attention given to *environmental* arguments, concerns of local residents and commercial arguments.

Sources of information should include articles and videos relating to the campaign of local Labour MP, John McDonnell and answers to his parliamentary questions. Statements by the incoming coalition government, in the Conservative and Liberal Democrat manifestos and in parliamentary statements, and press releases by Greenpeace and other related pressure groups.

C. Answering Exam Questions on the Environment

See section D in Liberalism for general advice about answering 10 and 30 mark questions.

The Ten Mark Question

Topic 4 Environmentalism

01   What is the difference between 'light' and 'bright' green thinking? (10 marks)

Again, this is a "compare and contrast" ten marker so we need to define both terms, highlight key differences and explain any controversies or points of interest.

Here we go!

Environmental politics are diverse, and the shades of opinion within the broad movement are often characterised in terms of their shade of green ("light green", "dark green", "bright green", etc.)

Mainstream environmentalists are generally considered to be "light green" – relatively moderate (compared with "dark green" ideas), their proposals involve only minor, manageable and electorally-acceptable changes in lifestyle and policy. "Light green" thinkers will champion greater use of public transport, energy-saving light-bulbs, cycling to work, turning things off "stand-by", recycling more of our waste, etc. alongside challenging but achievable targets relating to carbon emissions, pollution, etc.

This position has been traditionally criticised – in a rather pessimistic and apocalyptic, "we're all doomed" fashion – by "dark green" thinkers. But "bright green" thinkers offer an alternative vision. Their "brightness" is down to their optimism. "Bright green" thinkers believe that modern technology can be harnessed and used to make genuine, large-scale changes – eclipsing the small life-style changes of the "light green" brigade. Through this they believe we *can* stop global warming and save the planet. They point to renewable energy sources, carbon capture and clean coal technology, innovations in "green" science and technology. They believe that if governments invest in these areas, there is every reason to be optimistic about the future.

Both "light" and "bright" green thinkers are dismissed as overly-optimistic (at best) by the radical "dark green" ones.

Let's consider a different type of 10 mark question:

Topic 4	The Environment
01	What is meant by the term 'sustainable development'? (10 marks)

This is a more straight-forward "definition plus" question. To answer it, you would use an extended explanation and definition, like that given in the glossary below. However, it also helps to *contextualise* your answer – so give a good example. You could point to investment in "green jobs" and green technology; you could consider whether "eco-tourism" was a good alternative to traditional forms of development in some developing countries, etc.

The Thirty Mark Question (8)

Topic 4	Environment
02	"We're all green now." Discuss (30 marks)

Using this section, your class notes, the A2 Ideologies website and other sources, attempt this question in full. Then check the planned "model answer" at the end of this book. Make notes of key differences between your answer and the suggested model answer. Make sure you make note of things that you did not include that you might have done, but also ensure that you note what is not included in the model answer that might have been. Feel free to comment on this on the A2 Ideologies website.

D. Environment Glossary

Bright Green

Bright green refers to those environmentalists who have an optimistic and achievable set of proposals for dealing with the environmental crisis, via science and new technology. Bright green environmentalists will focus on the possibilities of renewable energy sources, will argue for clean coal technology, carbon neutral technology, power from wind, water and tide: large-scale technological solutions to the crisis. They are "bright" because they are optimistic. Some critics would suggest that they are two optimistic – that they have too much faith in the possibilities of the new technologies they champion. Others point out that there are vested interests at play in some of the green industries and question whether they are all as environmentally friendly as they purport to be. These industries might be accused of being "lite green" – meaning that their "greenness" is all about marketing and not about substance.

Dark Green

Dark green essentially refers to the most radical "greens" and describes an ideology that does not recognise the "quick fixes" of bright green people, nor the small-scale lifestyle changes championed by the light greens. For dark greens, the lifestyle changes have to be absolute and fundamental. Governments have to be cured of their "growthmania" – growth is a bad thing. For dark greens, we need to take steps backwards; why develop electric cars when you can simply abolish cars? We need to get back to nature and change our lives.

Development

Development is a contested term. It is often measured in purely economic terms – countries with a high GDP (gross domestic product) are considered *developed*. However, such a definition ignores inequality, quality of life and impact on the environment. If all countries were to develop the way the UK did (for example) there would be an environmental catastrophe. Therefore people increasingly talk about *sustainable* development.

Ecologism

Ecologism is the name sometimes given to a whole ideology of the environment (usually a "dark green" one) that cannot merely be an "add-on" to other ideologies: ecologism is a distinct ideology, in opposition to conservatism, liberalism and traditional socialism. When the term is used in this way, it is generally contrasted with *environmentalism*. David Cameron can profess to be an environmentalist while remaining a conservative all the while; he could not do the same and claim to support ecologism.

Ecology

Ecology is different from ecologism (and hence there is potential confusion with the word "ecologist"). Ecology is the scientific study of the environment, and therefore an ecologist in an environmental scientist, rather than a "dark green" ideologue.

Environmentalism

Environmentalism is a broad, catch-all term for those political/ideological views that have a particular concern for the environment. While environmentalism has come to be seen as mostly referring to global warming, carbon emissions, etc. it is also the politics of smaller-scale environmental matters like wildlife protection, conservation and animal rights. Environmentalism is sometimes contrasted with ecologism. When it is, environmentalism is presented as the more moderate, "lighter" approach, compared with the "darker", more ideological ecologism. Ecologism is an ideology in itself, whereas liberals, socialists and conservatives could also be environmentalists.

Green

"Green" is a very general label attached to all environmentalist or ecological politics. Many countries now have Green parties, as well as green pressure groups and social movements.

Light Green

Light green refers to moderate approaches to environmental politics. Much green thinking within mainstream politics tends to be "light" rather than "dark" green and looks at ways in which environmental protection can go hand in hand with rather subtle, small changes to our lifestyles and activities. Driving less, recycling more, using energy-saving lightbulbs and not leaving things on standby; all are considered worthy but decidedly "light" by those who approach this from a "darker" perspective.

Sustainable Development

Sustainable development refers to a way in which a country or an area can develop economically, without having a negative impact on the environment. For example, sustainable forestry involves replacing felled trees with newly planted ones; industry based on renewable energy sources where waste can be recycled or reprocessed is also more sustainable. "Dark green" thinkers would suggest that sustainable development is still rooted in "growthmania" and misses the point: economic growth is destroying the planet – finding sustainable and renewable ways to grow just means we are destroying the planet more slowly

PART THREE: REVISION AND EXAM TECHNIQUES AND TOP TIPS

REVISION TECHNIQUES

How do you revise?

If your answer is that you just read through your notes (or read through a textbook or revision guide) then you are not maximising your chances of fulfilling your potential and getting those high grades. That is not to say you will not get a high grade revising that way – some people undoubtedly do – but the revision probably did not play that big a part in getting the grade!

And let's face it, you spend an awfully long time revising, so it makes sense to use that time in the most effective and efficient way possible.

First of all, make sure you have a revision timetable. Teachers will have mentioned it and you might have decided to ignore them! Don't! It's really important to plan when you are going to revise all your subjects and ensure that you give all of them the appropriate amount of time. If you do not do this, then the chances are you will revise for your first exam first, then for your second, etc. potentially leaving you with very little time to revise for some exams.

Timetable "down time" and leisure activities in your revision plan. If you say that you are going to spend every hour of every day revising Ideologies, you will not keep to your timetable, and then you might as well not have written one. If you know that you will watch Eastenders, and you do want to go out with your friends on Friday night, then include that in your timetable. You are much more likely to do the two hours you planned after Eastenders if watching it was in your plan!

Revise in an active way. Do something. Reading your notes, or this textbook, might well trigger a few memories and help a little. But the exam is not going to ask you what you can remember about Politics. It isn't a trivia quiz. Therefore it is much more useful to revise material in the way that you are going to use it in the exam.

Active Revision Methods:

- *Mindmaps or "Brainstorms"*. Take *either* a topic *or* a question and *mindmap* it. Connect themes, people, facts and arguments to one another across a large, blank sheet of paper. You might want to do this with notes at first, and later without notes, almost as a test. Through this method, you go over what you have learned (and perhaps test yourself on it) but, almost more importantly, you *make connections* and *see* how things are *connected*. Doing this with past-paper questions is particularly exam-focused revision.

- *Exam practice*. You can't really beat exam practice. Doing exactly what you will eventually have to do in the exam is the best way to prepare for it. It is likely that teachers will be prepared to mark these practice answers, but you can also use the exam board's published mark schemes to mark them yourself.

- *Tests and Quizzes*. If you have read through your notes, do not just assume that you have remembered it. Get other people in your group to quiz you on the relevant topics. Setting questions for others can also be an effective way of going through your notes in an active way.

- *Record your notes*. This is a bit out of leftfield, but you could record yourself reading your notes (or record your teacher talking in a revision session, with their permission!) and listen to these recordings in the car, before you go to bed, in the bath, etc. The repetition *might* help.

- *Condense your notes*. Less unusually, many people re-write their notes. Personally, I can't see much advantage to simply writing the notes again in exactly the same form (although everybody learns things differently) – what might be more useful is to condense notes into "revision guide" form. In other words, take a topic area that might be five or six pages in your notes and try and *condense* it into a single page, including all the essential information.

- *Post-it notes*. Another unusual suggestion that some students have reported favourably is sticking post-it notes all around your room (and possibly your house) with key points, facts and quotations on them. That way, when you get milk from the fridge, you might read that Herbert Morrison said that "Socialism is whatever the Labour Party happens to be doing at the time".

Everybody has their own favourite revision techniques. Discuss it with your group – somebody might have one that would really suit you too. Some people colour code all their notes, others just rely on reading the textbook. Everybody is different, but the more active the revision method, and the closer the skill involved is to those needed in the exam, by far the better.

EXAM TECHNIQUES

What do you do in the exam?

Hopefully you didn't answer, "panic!" The first and most important thing is to the read the paper very carefully. You should be fully aware of the style of the paper before you get there, but read the instructions again and be clear what you have to do. You have to select two topics and answer both the questions in each of those topics.

Choosing your topics

Hopefully, you begin the exam with a full choice of topics available to you. Of course some people decide "I'm not doing fascism" or "I'm not doing the economy", but if you are one of those people, do bear in mind the extent to which this reduces your *choice* in the exam.

Initially try and make your choice based on the 30-mark essay questions. This is where the bulk of the marks are located so it makes complete sense to base your choices on these questions. Of course you might like (or dislike!) two 30-mark questions equally and, here, you might use the 10 mark question as a discriminator. However, my general advice would be to choose a topic by the 30-mark question *even if you are very unhappy with the 10 mark question.*

Answering the questions

Consider the option of answering the 30-mark questions first. Providing you number your answer-book properly and clearly there is absolutely no problem with this. People are often scared of doing it, but it is amazing how often people report having run out of time to finish their second essay. If you really can't bear to do it, or if you feel like the ten-markers serve as a limbering-up exercise for the big questions, stick to your usual routine. But starting with the essay questions can really help from a time management point of view.

Really important – make a plan. The thirty-mark questions, though shorter than A2 questions of the past, should not just be started without a plan. You need to know where you are going and what you are going to try and include. This does not need to be a long, detailed plan. On your answer-book, do a quick "mindmap" or "brainstorm" to ensure that you have remembered all the relevant information. Either "brainstorm" this into "for" and "against" columns (if appropriate) or number the points before you start writing, to show the order you are going to address them in the essay. Consider ticking them off as you have addressed them. Make sure the plan is legible for the examiner to look at should they wish to – you might pick up some marks (as such, do not cross it out).

Time Management

Time management is really important. It can be very frustrating in some A Level exams, especially at AS, when it seems almost as though the exam is testing how fast students can write, rather than their understanding of the topics. However, with a clear idea of how much time is available for each question, it should be possible to answer these questions with reasonable comfort.

There are eighty marks available, and ninety minutes in the exam. Assuming it might take approximately five minutes to read the paper and choose the questions (hopefully it might take a little less) you will then have roughly a "mark a minute", followed by five minutes at the end to read through your answers and make necessary corrections and changes. If you tackle both 30-mark questions first, you should be getting close to having finished the second one when an hour has passed. If you are into the last 20 minutes and you have not started the ten-mark questions, then you are running behind time. Quick measures like this can be very helpful.

If you finish, do not sit back or (worse) leave. Read through what you have written, carefully. You have been writing quickly, so you will *always* have made one or two careless errors, or expressed something in a way that you might like to improve on. Too many students miss out on that important opportunity to improve their work.

SELECT BIBLIOGRAPHY / RECOMMENDED READING

Benn, Tony *Arguments for Socialism* (Jonathan Cape, 1979)

Giddens, Anthony *The Third Way* (Polity Press, 1999)

Gilroy, Paul *There Ain't No Black in the Union Jack* (Routledge, 1987)

Green, E.H.H *The Crisis of Conservatism* (Routledge, 1994)

Losurdo, Domenico *Liberalism: A Counter History* (Verso, 2011)

Mill, John Stuart *On Liberty and Other Essays* (Oxford University Press 1991)

Riff, M.A (ed) *Dictionary of Modern Political Ideologies* (Manchester University Press, 1987)

Rousseau, Jean-Jacques *The Social Contract* (Penguin Classics, 1968)

Williams, Raymond *Keywords: A Vocabulary of Culture and Society* (Fontana, 1976)

MODEL ANSWER PLANS

Thirty Mark Question 1:

"We're all liberals now." Discuss

- What is the question asking? Can we *rephrase* it? If "we're all liberals now" this suggests that liberalism is the *dominant ideology* and that all the main parties follow the liberal ideology. This then is how to approach the question. To *discuss* it, it is often easiest to simply put *two* sides to the case: a) we *are* all liberals now, b) we're not!

- Paragraph one – *Introduction*. Decode the question (as above). Give some indication as to how the argument is going to progress and what sort of evidence you are going to use in order to pursue this argument.

- Paragraph two – *"We're all liberals now"*. This paragraph (or section – it may stretch over a few paragraphs) is the case for the *defence* of the proposition in the questions.
  - Key principles of liberalism. There is a liberal *hegemony* in Britain today – these key principles are accepted by most people. (Some opportunity to discuss key thinkers, though don't go off on a tangent)
  - The main parties are all liberal:
    - Is the Conservative Party liberal? Remember the different *types* of liberalism. Conservative Party is committed to *economic* liberalism in particular, but you may have other examples of Conservative liberalism from Chapter 2, part c.
    - Is the Labour Party liberal? Again, remember the different *types* of liberalism. Focus on *social liberalism* but also interest in constitutional reform, and some examples of economic liberalism
    - The Liberal Democrat Party is, probably, quite liberal! But again, consider the different *types* of liberalism.

- Paragraph (or section) three – *"We're not all liberals now!"* Here we consider the arguments *against* the proposition in the question

  - Existence of other ideologies (socialism, conservatism, even fascism) that are defined, at least in part, by their *difference* from liberalism

  - The main parties are *not* entirely liberal:

    - The Conservative Party *isn't* liberal? Although there is a commitment to *economic* liberalism, in other ways modern conservatism could be seen to be illiberal. Consider *social* or *positive* liberalism and relate to welfare reform, tuition fees, etc. Also consider *authoritarian* aspects of conservatism.

    - The Labour Party *isn't* liberal? Consider the Labour Party's approach to anti-terror legislation – authoritarian. Also Labour's response to the economic crisis was economically illiberal. Consider arguments that Labour has a "big state" approach to politics.

    - The Liberal Democrats aren't liberal? Really? Had they abandoned classical liberalism in favour of social democracy? Have the new Orange Book liberals in the coalition government abandoned social liberalism?

- Paragraph (or section) four: *Conclusion.* Is liberalism the dominant ideology in Britain today? There are arguments to suggest that it is, although this is helped by there being such different, almost contradictory varieties of liberalism to choose from! Socialism and conservatism are not dead, but the modern versions of both have accepted most of the key tenets of liberalism. Although fascists continue to reject liberalism, they are a small minority, and even they have chosen to focus on liberal issues like freedom of speech in recent years.

You need to ensure that you have plenty of *real examples* when discussing policies, etc. If you have produced the policy files recommended in this book, then you should be able to do this with ease. Remember to use the accompanying website to help with this further.

Thirty Mark Question 2:

"The Labour Party is a democratic socialist party" Discuss.

- What is the question asking? Can we rephrase it? The quotation comes from Clause IV of the *current* Labour Party constitution – let them know that you know that! However, the question is really: how socialist is the Labour Party?

- *Introduction* – Decode the question as above. Indicate how the argument is going to develop. The simplest way to address this question is to firstly outline the various arguments that suggest that the Labour Party *is* socialist and, secondly, to challenge those arguments with those that suggest it is not, followed by a conclusion. You could, of course, do it the other way around and that might work better, as the non-traditional, "revisionist" socialism might work better in the second half. There's no *right* way to do it, so long as you ensure that you constantly address the question you have been asked.

- *Section one – The Labour Party is NOT socialist*
    - Tony Benn said "the Labour Party has never been a socialist party but it has always had socialists in it"
    - It might have been socialist at the start, or in Attlee's time, with the creation of the Welfare State and the NHS, but by the advent of New Labour, socialism was no longer part of the party's ideology
    - The quotation comes from the "new" Clause IV, but in many ways that document spelt out the end of socialism in the party. It removed the old Clause IV which committed the party to "common ownership" and instead praised the "rigours of competition" and the "dynamism of the market". This committed the Labour Party to capitalism and, as socialism is an ideology fundamentally opposed to capitalism, stopped the Labour Party from being a socialist party.
    - The Labour governments of Blair and Brown were very close to *business* (give examples – e.g. Bernie Ecclestone affair) and were not ideologically opposed to inequality (give example of Peter Mandelson being "intensely comfortable" with people becoming "filthy rich" under a Labour government) – at the same time they sometimes seemed hostile to unions, and certainly didn't revoke Thatcher's anti-union legislation.

- Come to mention it, they didn't reverse any of Thatcher or Major's privatisations either, and did some privatising of their own (e.g. Air Traffic Control)

- Blair's government also engaged in wars in Afghanistan and Iraq, in coalition with a very right-wing US administration and in opposition to many moderate and left-wing voices world-wide.

- New Labour also introduced private finance into various public services

- In these respects, Labour in government since 1997 could be seen as *New Right* – hardly socialist or even social democratic! They *say* they're socialist, but this seems to tie in with Herbert Morrison (Peter Mandelson's grandfather) who said that "socialism is whatever the Labour Party happens to be doing at the time" – a singularly unhelpful definition!

- Since 2010, Ed Miliband has signalled the "death" of New Labour, but not the rebirth of socialism! His opposition to strikes by public sector workers in 2011 showed that he had not strayed far from the ideological position of Blair and Brown.

- *Section Two – The Labour Party IS socialist*

  - Modern democratic socialism is not the same as the revolutionary or extreme socialisms of the past. It is not an ideology that seeks to end capitalism and replace it, nor is it an ideology that will give knee-jerk support to every strike.

  - Since the 1950s, British democratic socialism has moved on from an argument about nationalisation and state control of the economy, to being one about *equality*, fairness and social inclusion.

  - New Labour in government introduced the minimum wage – something no previous Labour government had managed to do.

  - New Labour in government managed to invest vast sums of money in health and education

  - New Labour's foreign wars were for humanitarian intervention – against brutal dictators; socialists went to fight Franco in the Spanish Civil War, why not fight Saddam Hussain? (*Feel free to add some evaluation here – never be scared of multiple "howevers"!*)

- Labour responded to the banking crisis by investing huge sums of money and, indeed, by nationalising some banks! (*Another however – the Party seemed ashamed of nationalising banks and insisted that they'd be returned to private ownership as soon as possible – hardly confident old-style socialism!*)

- *Conclusion* This all comes down to one's definition of "democratic socialism". If, by that term, we take an "Old" Labour left definition, meaning a democratic path to socialism, including public ownership and control, internationalism, support for trade unions and opposition to capitalism – then, no, the modern Labour Party is not a democratic socialist party (though it still has democratic socialists in it, like John McDonnell and left-wing groups like the Labour Representation Committee). However, if we accept that the meaning of "democratic socialist" has changed in the UK, as the Labour Party has changed – essentially accepting Herbert Morrison's case that "socialism is whatever the Labour Party happens to be doing at the time" then, perhaps the Labour Party is still a democratic socialist party. However, if Labour Party socialism is now about equality, fairness and social inclusion, there is still a case to be made that New Labour in government failed to live up to this revisionist version of democratic socialism as well!

Thirty Mark Question 3:

To what extent has the ideology of the Conservative Party changed since 1997?

- What is the question asking? Can we rephrase it? The question is asking us about quite a limited time period, so we should not waste time on conservative ideologies of previous eras. Essentially, we're looking at how the Conservative Party changed in opposition. We don't have to just say how the ideology of David Cameron's conservatives differs from that of John Major's – we can consider changes between those dates too (did the ideology change under William Hague, Ian Duncan-Smith or Michael Howard?) For ease of structuring the *argument* it might be easiest to consider this in terms of a) arguments that the Conservative Party's underlying ideology has changed a good deal in that time against b) the core ideology of the Conservative Party remains largely unchanged.

- *Introduction*. Decode/rephrase the question and set out where the argument is going, as above

- *Section One – The ideology of the Conservative Party has changed since 1997*
    - Labour landslide in 1997, defeated a Conservative Party still wedded to Thatcherite, New Right ideology (and divided over the European Union)
    - Although changes under Hague, Duncan-Smith and Howard were subtle (in terms of *ideology* – they did bring in structural reforms to the party) David Cameron's conservatism is very different to that of John Major and his Thatcherite cabinet
    - Thatcherite ideology: "there is no such thing as society" vs. Cameron: The Big Society
    - Major – back to basics; "cricket and warm beer" – Cameron's conservatism is more *modern* and 21st century
    - Labour in 1997 promised to "save the NHS"; David Cameron promised that his priorities were "N. H. S"
    - Europe has ceased to be a bone of contention and is no longer "toxic" for the party (*however… vote on EU referendum in 2011*)
    - Comfortably entered coalition with a left-of-centre Liberal Democrat party
- *Section Two – the ideology of the Conservative Party remains unchanged*
    - Although *policies* have changed, the underlying ideology has not
    - Thatcher's "there is no such thing as society" is ultimately the same as Cameron's "there is such a thing as society, but it is not the same as the state".
    - Cameron's priorities were "N H S" but the coalition government's *policies* were a radical reform, more radical than anything Thatcher or Major attempted
    - Europe has become less of an issue because the party has become a more united eurosceptic, Thatcherite party. In other words, the party has consolidated its Thatcherite position and is less ideologically diverse than in 1997 (despite the presence of europhile Kenneth Clarke and a handful of Liberal Democrats around the Cabinet table)
    - Cameron's ideological speeches (such as 2009 conference speech) show deep commitment to neoliberal economics and neoconservative social policy: he is of the New Right. So were Howard, Duncan-Smith, Hague and Major.
    - Changes then have been in terms of *rebranding*, not changing the ideology (e.g. "lite" green presentation)

- *Conclusion* Make sure it follows on logically from the beginning. You could argue that Major had more elements of one nation and traditional conservatism in his ideological makeup (with his warm beer and cricket) and that David Cameron is more classically Thatcherite! You could suggest that the party initially swung to the right with Hague, Duncan-Smith and Howard and has now returned to an ideological position similar to that of Major's party. You could argue that the Conservative Party has returned to being a party of the very rich and privileged (pointing to the socio-economic background of top Tories today, compared with Thatcher, Major, Hague, etc.) All of these would be reasonable conclusions, providing they are backed up and follow on logically from what came before.

Thirty Mark Question 4:

"Fascism is primarily identified by what it *opposes* rather than what it supports." Discuss

- What is the question asking? Can we rephrase it? The question appears to be suggesting that fascism is not a coherent ideology, but rather a *reaction* to other ideologies, events, etc. In order to discuss this, we are going to have to first of all look at the extent to which fascism *is* defined by what it opposes, and secondly see if we can identify some key *proposals* of fascist ideology.

- *Introduction.* Decode or rephrase the question and then set out where this argument is going (as above)

- *Section One: fascism IS all about what it opposes.*

  - Italian and German fascism were reactions against:

    - *Ideologies* – Fascists saw liberalism and socialism as dangerous ideologies. The class interests and internationalism of socialism undermined the nation; the democracy and pluralism of liberalism threatened unity and strong leadership

    - *Events* - Fascists were also greatly influenced by historical events, following the First World War. The Nazis in Germany, for instance, saw their defeat as a national humiliation, and the penalties placed on them by the victors as unjust. Fascists in Italy, Germany and elsewhere were not only opposed to socialism as an ideology but also to the activities of socialists and communists in their countries

- o *Reason* – Fascists also reacted against the growth of reason, science and logic. These were threats against instinct, and emotions like *anger*, *loyalty* and *revenge* – all of which were important aspects of political motivation

- ▪ In other ways, fascist movements around the world have been quite *different*. So, for example, Nazism was focused on issues of race; Italian and German fascism favoured corporatist economics while South American fascism preferred neo-liberalism, etc. From this perspective, the aspects of fascism that appear common to all fascists are those areas of *opposition*: especially opposition to liberalism, socialism, communism and democracy.

- *Section Two – Fascism also has key proposals or ideas*

  - ▪ When Mussolini set out the principles of fascism, it was *not* just about what he disliked about contemporary Italian society and other ideologies: there were key ideas at the heart of fascism, many of which have already been referred to:

    - o *Nationalism.* Fascism has a strong and assertive sense of nationalism. Fascists believe that their nation should be powerful and dominant. Many of the other key elements of fascism are rooted in nationalism

    - o *Elitism.* The flipside of the fascist opposition to democracy is a positive support for *elitism*. They do believe that people require leadership and that a small group in society can lead the nation to great things

    - o *The Leader.* Fascists place a great deal of importance on a unifying figurehead who can lead the nation: a Caesar who people will follow.

    - o *Military Success and Expansion.* One of the key ways the nation can demonstrate its greatness is through successes on the battlefield and through conquest o *Totalitarianism.* Fascists believe in a totalitarian state, when all aspects of national life are controlled by the fascist state

  ■ *Section Three – Exceptions.* Of course, like any of the other ideologies we have discussed, there are varieties of fascism and not all fascists sign up to an identical manifesto. Nazi Germany had its anti-Semitism, Fascist Chile had its neo-liberal economic agenda, there were different degrees of totalitarianism.

  ■ *Conclusion.* Although fascism can be seen as a revolutionary form of *ultra-conservatism* it is identified by more than simply what it opposes. Like ultra-conservatism, it was opposed to the huge changes that industrialisation was having on Europe and on the dominant ideas in the continent. But it had quite a specific, novel agenda with which to combat these threats. It was not a movement that sought to merely re-establish the *ancien regimes* of pre-Enligtenment Europe; it favoured strong leadership and elitism, but had no allegiance to the aristocratic elites of the past. Fascism was something new.

Thirty Mark Question 5:

"Multiculturalism has failed." Discuss

- What is the question? Can we rephrase it? Clearly we will need to try and establish what multiculturalism is (not straightforward). Who argues that it *has* failed? We will need to analyse their claims. To frame this argument, we will need to consider arguments that it *has* failed, and contrast those with arguments that it has not.

- *Introduction*: Rephrase/decode the question, and say how the argument is going to develop (as above)

- *Section One*: *Multiculturalism has failed.*

  o Refer to David Cameron's comments on the subject

  o Similar concerns elsewhere in Europe; Sarkozy and the "burkha ban" in France

- What is the origin of the argument?
  - "Homegrown" terrorism
  - 7/7, radical preachers
  - Increased wearing of niqabs
  - Segregated communities
  - Race riots; particularly in northern mill towns and cities
  - More extreme concerns/arguments put across by people on far right – e.g. Geert Wilders in Holland, who warns of the "Islamification" of Europe
  - Growth of far-right, anti-immigration organisations like the BNP and EDL in the UK (and similar organisations across Europe)
  - Extreme acts like the Oslo bombing / shootings
- Cameron's argument is that multiculturalism was well-meaning, but the focus should have been on *integration* not on multiculturalism: people need a shared British identity
- *Section Two – Multiculturalism has* not *failed*
  - The above argument based on a misunderstanding of the concept of multiculturalism
  - The Oslo bombing / shootings, a protest against the *success* of multiculturalism in Norway, not its failure
  - No contradiction between multiculturalism and integration
  - Bans, like that in France, are *illiberal* and promote extremism (both right-wing extremism and extremism within minority communities) – leads to more separatism not more integration
  - Race riots and even terrorism, partly a result of *not enough multiculturalism* rather than too much: communities ignorant of each other: areas not multicultural enough!
  - It is the wrong response to groups like the BNP, EDL, French National Front, etc. to try and appease them. Multiculturalism should be proudly defended against extremists
- *Conclusion*
- This will clearly partly depend on your views (although make sure that your conclusions follow on logically from what went before). You might choose to agree with the thrust of the question, that multiculturalism was a well-meaning experiment that went wrong, or you can conclude that multiculturalism is a fact of modern society and cannot be blamed for terrorism or community conflict.

Thirty Mark Question 6:

"The educational policies of modern UK parties are deeply ideological." Discuss (30 marks)

- What is the question asking? Can we rephrase it? This is one of those questions that could be asked either way around: are the policies ideological, or are they more pragmatic? That is the best way to structure the argument: a) arguments to suggest that educational policy *is* deeply ideological; b) arguments to suggest it is more pragmatic.
- *Introduction.* Decode / rephrase the question and indicate where the argument is going, as above.
- *Educational policy is deeply ideological*
    - o Take this on a party-by-party basis!
    - o Conservative Party
        - What policies can we discuss?
        - Free schools and academies – fits in with New Right ideology – small state and big society
        - Tuition fees of up-to £9000 – introduces a market into higher education; rolling back the state (massive reduction in state teaching grant)
    - o Liberal Democrats
        - At election (obvious change since!!) – removal of tuition fees – social liberal, positive freedom agenda
        - Pupil premium – social liberal approach
    - o Labour Party
        - Defending SureStart (compensatory education – egalitarian)
        - Opposing high fees – (egalitarian, however…)
        - Investing in infrastructure ("building schools for the future") – Keynesian, investment in economy
- *Educational policy is more pragmatic*
    - o Conservative Party

- - *They* would argue NOT ideological – their policies are what will work, or what is possible given the current economic situation

  o Liberal Democrats

    - Policies changed

    - HE funding – had already changed policy before election, to slow reduction in fees rather than immediate abolition (presented as pragmatic in light of economic problems)

    - Policies now what can be delivered by the coalition, rather than what they are ideologically committed too

  o Labour Party

    - Not sure about HE funding policy yet – not ideologically coherent, not least because they introduced fees and commissioned the report that came up with the new fees regime. Would they have taken a different view in government?

    - Free schools developed from Labour's own Academies programme

    - Internal debate in Labour about future policies; ideology is one driving force, but clearly electability is another one

- *Conclusion.* There are clear differences between the education policies of the three main parties but also a lot of overlap. The differences (apart from, before the election, on HE funding) are apparently quite slight ones, and appear to be based on pragmatic questions (is that policy *affordable*) rather than ideological ones. Either education policy *is* ideological, and all three parties are driven by a form of neoliberal ideology, or they are more pragmatic. Ensure your conclusion follows on logically from what has gone before.

Thirty Mark Question 7:

"There are now no significant differences between the economic policies of the main UK political parties." Discuss (30 marks)

- What is the question asking? Can we rephrase it? It is looking for significant ideological differences between the main parties in terms of economic policy. It is asking about *now* rather than the past, so we need to focus on contemporary policy. The easiest way to structure this question (as usual, with the "discuss" question) will be to consider the two "sides" of the argument: a) there *are* now *no* significant differences between the economic policies and b) there are differences. Because the economic crises of the last few years have exposed some apparently significant differences in economic policy, it might on this occasion work better to *start* with the argument that there *are* significant differences.

- *Introduction*: Decode / rephrase the question and set out where the argument is going to go (as above)

- *Section One – there* are *significant differences between the economic policies of the main UK parties*

    o Approaches to the banking crisis

        ▪ Conservative Party – laissez-faire (accused of being the "do nothing" party); opposed to nationalisations of banks; prefer a market-oriented response

        ▪ Liberal Democrat Party – at the time, led by Vince Cable, strong argument for state intervention and nationalisations

        ▪ Labour Party – closer to Liberal Democrat position, although reluctant to nationalise; tried to remain "hands-off"

    o Approaches to recession

        ▪ Labour Party – high levels of public spending (and borrowing); investment in infrastructure and in trying to create jobs. Argued that spending had to continue until growth was fully established, before cuts could be made to deal with the deficit

        ▪ Liberal Democrat Party - Before the General Election, very similar approach to the recession to Labour. After the election argued that deficit was too severe and had to be addressed immediately

        ▪ Conservative Party – neoliberal opposition to interventions by Labour Party; argued for tight grip on spending; after election – argued strongly for deep and immediate cuts in public spending

    o Other aspects of economic policy

        ▪ Conservative Party – wants to "rebalance" the economy away from large public sector; wants to see growth in private sector and manufacturing

        ▪ Other parties have not expressed clear opposition to this aspiration, but clearly the Labour Party grew the *public* sector significantly when it was in power.

        ▪ General approach – Labour & Lib Dem: Keynesian; Conservative: monetarist and laissez-faire.

- *There are now no significant differences*

- o Despite these apparent big differences, the economic *ideologies* of the parties are closer than ever.

    - All parties committed to capitalism, to free-market economics and enterprise (see Labour's new clause IV)

    - Three "pro-business" parties

    - Three parties committed to relatively low levels of taxation, minimal government intervention in the economy; prefer private ownership to public ownership

    - Even when Labour nationalised some banks, it did so apologetically and with clear commitments to return them to private ownership as soon as possible (despite possible advantages to maintaining public ownership for longer)

    - All three parties promised "deep" and "savage" cuts to public spending – the differences were slight and based largely on *timing*

    - Ed Miliband criticised public-sector strikes; spoke at TUC anti-cuts demonstration, but still committed to deep public spending cuts

- *Conclusion*. Ensure this follows logically from what has gone before. It is hard to ignore the points made in the first section: clearly the parties (especially Labour and Conservatives) had *very* different responses to economic crisis, and this appears rooted in their different ideological perspectives. However, over a longer period of time, there does appear to have been a neoliberal consensus. Has that been damaged for good? Or are we likely to find ourselves back in a period of neo-liberal consensus once the economy finally starts to get back on track?

Thirty Mark Question 8:

"We're all greens now." Discuss (30 marks)

- What is the question asking? Can we rephrase it? This essay, a bit like the "we're all liberals now" one, asks us to investigate the extent to which all the main UK political parties have accepted the green or environmental agenda, and adopted "green" policies.

- *Introduction* Decode the question, as above. Give some indication as to where the argument is going. The easiest way to "discuss" in an essay is to explore two "sides": a) we *are* all greens now; (b) we're not.

- *Section One - We are all greens now.*

  - Big environmental issues, like global warming, are so big and of such general concern that all the main political parties are talking about them, not just the Green Party.

  - Include a summary of some current policies and commitments at the 2010 general election.

  - All parties committed to "bright green" approach of investing in "green jobs".

  - No mainstream party in the UK questions general thrust of green agenda or publically doubts data about global warming.

  - All parties committed to international agreements (Kyoto and Copenhagen) and indeed to going beyond those targets.

  - Lib Dems seen as most green of mainstream parties, but even the Conservative Party is now "green". (Talk about Cameron's "greening" of the Party).

- *Section Two - We're not all green now!*

  - Question the ideological commitment to a green agenda of *any* of the parties. Take them in turn:

  - Are the Conservatives merely "lite green" – using green language and imagery for marketing reasons? What have they really done?

  - Labour and Lib Dems talk green, but – from a "dark green" perspective, they are found seriously wanting. They are obsessed with *growth*. They are interested in making growth more *sustainable* and in finding alternatives to resources that are being greatly depleted, but only in order to maintain capitalism, industrialism and growthmania. They are not committed to a different sort of society, in harmony with nature. Evidence? Look at Labour's determination to build a third runway at Heathrow. Even those parties that didn't want to build it put forward alternatives elsewhere – they didn't challenge the logic that we need more air travel. In the end it was a victim of budget cuts, not of green thinking.

Conclusion – Perhaps, rather than all being green now, all the main parties recognise that there is electoral advantage to be gained by paying lip service to light green ideas? However, you could argue that all three main political parties are now quite serious in their bright green agendas? Or are they again just using green language to sell their economic agendas? (*In the end, your conclusion should include your view – following on logically from what has gone before in the argument*)

INDEX

11+, 107, 108, 109, 115, 116

1944 Education Act, 110, 114, 127

1997 General Election, 24, 44, 69, 98

Abbott, Diane, 94

anarchist, 11

aristocracy, 13, 60, 63, 73, 88, 110

Attlee, Clement, 43, 159

authoritarian, 11, 73, 158

Benn, Tony, 9, 38, 44, 45, 56, 62, 68, 126, 132, 156, 159

Bentham, Jeremy, 15, 16, 26, 37

Bevan, Aneurin, 43, 44, 46, 77

Beveridge, William, 21, 43

Big Society, 22, 26, 51, 73, 162

Blair, Tony, 9, 23, 28, 43, 49, 50, 51, 56, 67, 68, 69, 82, 98, 119, 125, 129, 134, 159, 160

Blunkett, David, 95

BNP. See British National Party, See British National Party, See British National Party, See British National Party, See British National Party, See British National Party, See British National Party, See British National Party, See British National Party, See British National Party, See British National Party, See British National Party, See British National Party, See British National Party

bright green, 143, 145, 150, 171

British National Party, 78

Brown, Gordon, 26, 68, 82, 96, 112, 113, 129, 134, 138, 139, 159, 160

Burke, Edmund, 59, 63

burkha, 92, 165

Butler, Rab, 110, 114

Callaghan, James, 82, 110, 111

Cameron, David, 26, 27, 50, 61, 62, 63, 66, 67, 68, 73, 83, 84, 91, 93, 99, 110, 112, 125, 126, 127, 144, 145, 150, 161, 162, 163, 165, 166, 171

Campbell, Menzies, 119

Churchill, Winston, 42, 80

civil rights, 14, 35, 36, 37, 94

Clarke, Kenneth, 62, 112, 162

Clause IV, 41, 43, 45, 49, 57, 159

Clegg, Nick, 21, 22, 68

climate change, 141, 143, 144

Communist, 38, 40, 46, 56, 78, 94

Conservative Party, 10, 19, 21, 22, 25, 26, 27, 28, 50, 51, 52, 60, 61, 62, 64, 65, 66, 67, 68, 69, 70, 73, 74, 83, 96, 99, 101, 107, 110, 112, 116, 121, 127, 129, 133, 144, 145, 146, 157, 158, 161, 162, 163, 167, 169, 171

corporatism, 78, 82, 133

Crosland, Tony, 57, 110, 116, 119

Dark green, 143, 150, 151

Davies, David, 27, 68

Disability Discrimination Act, 23

Disraeli, Benjamin, 61, 65

ecologism, 142, 150

EDL, 80, 81, 166

Education Reform Act, 117, 126

egalitarian, 35, 110, 116, 126, 141, 167

Enlightenment, 13, 35, 75

Equality Act, 23

European Union, 51, 73, 96, 138, 162

Fabian Society, 39, 48, 56

fascism, 5, 11, 75, 76, 77, 78, 79, 80, 81, 82, 83, 84, 85, 88, 154, 158, 163, 164, 165

Feminism, 96, 104

Foot, Michael, 44

free market, 11, 15, 23, 26, 36, 37, 65, 67, 118, 128, 138, 142

free schools, 121

Freedom of Information Act, 23

French Revolution, 14, 15, 36, 59, 63

Friedman, Milton, 65, 130, 131, 133, 134, 138, 139

Gadaffi, 78

Gaitskell, Hugh, 43, 44, 46

globalisation, 132, 138

Goldsmith, Zac, 144

Gove, Michael, 111, 121

Gramsci, Antonio, 36

Green Party, 141, 146, 171

Greenpeace, 140, 146

Griffin, Nick, 80, 81

Hardie, Keir, 38

Healey, Denis, 44

Heseltine, Michael, 62

Hitler, Adolf, 11, 75, 76, 77, 79, 80, 88, 89

Howard, Michael, 62, 83, 112, 161, 162, 163

Human Rights Act, 23

Hussain, Saddam, 9, 160

ID cards, 25, 27

integration, 93, 95, 105, 166

Iraq War, 28, 51

Jenkins, Roy, 24

Keynes
    John Maynard, 138

Keynes, John Maynard, 21, 26, 130, 133, 134

Keynesian, 25, 130, 133, 134, 167, 169

Kinnock, Neil, 44, 46, 68, 69

Klu Klux Klan, 80, 94

Labour
    Party, 126, 138

Labour Party, 19, 21, 23, 24, 28, 39, 40, 41, 42, 43, 44, 45, 46, 48, 49, 51, 52, 56, 57, 62, 68, 69, 76, 80, 82, 98, 101, 112, 113, 133, 142, 145, 146, 154, 157, 158, 159, 160, 161, 167, 168, 169

Labour Representation Committee, 19, 40, 45, 46, 161

laissez-faire, 18, 20, 26, 28, 36, 42, 50, 61, 65, 73, 128, 134, 169

Lansbury, George, 42

liberal. See liberalism

Liberal Democrats, 10, 21, 27, 28, 48, 51, 52, 68, 69, 70, 80, 113, 141, 144, 158, 162, 167, 168

liberalism, 4, 9, 13, 14, 15, 16, 18, 19, 21, 23, 25, 27, 28, 30, 32, 33, 34, 35, 36, 37, 38, 52, 56, 59, 60, 65, 66, 69, 73, 74, 75, 76, 79, 80, 84, 142, 150, 157, 158, 163, 164

light green, 143, 145, 171

Lloyd George, David, 21

Lucas, Caroline, 146

MacDonald, Ramsay, 41, 42

Major, 62, 68, 93, 129, 134, 160, 161, 162, 163

Malthus, Thomas, 15

Mandela, Nelson, 11

Marx, Karl, 13, 15, 35, 38, 39, 56, 57, 76

Marxism, 15, 38, 56

Marxist, 9, 15, 36, 39, 40, 43, 47, 104

McDonnell, John, 46, 161

meritocracy, 35, 56, 73, 107, 108, 125, 126

Miliband, Ed, 45, 113, 160, 170

Mill, John Stuart, 16, 19, 34, 35, 37, 156

minimum wage, 24, 49, 132, 134, 160

Morris, William, 39, 46, 57

Morrison, Herbert, 57, 129, 154, 160, 161

Moseley, Oswald, 77

multiculturalism, 84, 91, 92, 93, 95, 105, 165, 166

Mussolini, Benito, 75, 76, 77, 79, 88, 89, 164

National Curriculum, 117, 118

National Front, 77, 78, 81, 166

National Health Service, 43, 50, 65

nationalisation, 41, 42, 49, 54, 57, 129, 160

Nazism, 77, 79, 80, 84, 88, 164

New Labour, 10, 23, 24, 43, 44, 45, 47, 48, 49, 50, 51, 52, 57, 58, 62, 68, 69, 119, 120, 134, 159, 160, 161

New Right, 9, 21, 50, 51, 62, 65, 66, 67, 68, 69, 73, 117, 118, 125, 130, 139, 160, 162, 167

Obama, Barack, 94, 95

orange book, 21, 28

Osborne, George, 26, 68, 134

Paine, Thomas, 14, 16

Peterloo, 14, 60

Powell, Enoch, 77, 83, 84, 94

public ownership, 39, 54, 56, 69, 73, 128, 129, 134, 161, 170

Race Relations Act, 94

racism, 77, 79, 81, 82, 84, 88, 91, 94, 104

Reagan, Ronald, 65, 66

Rousseau, Jean-Jacques, 14, 16, 34, 35, 37, 156

RSPB, 140, 146

slave trade, 15, 60, 64, 74

Smith, Adam, 18, 35, 36, 68, 134, 161, 162, 163

social contract, 14, 16, 35

social democracy, 21, 45, 47, 51, 52, 158

socialism, 4, 9, 10, 21, 38, 39, 40, 41, 42, 44, 45, 46, 47, 49, 50, 51, 53, 56, 57, 62, 75, 79, 80, 88, 129, 150, 158, 159, 160, 161, 163, 164

Socialist Campaign Group of Labour MPs, 10

Stalin, Joseph, 10, 11, 46, 89, 128

Surestart, 24

Tatchell, Peter, 84

Tebbit, Norman, 92

Thatcher
Margaret, 126

Thatcher, Margaret, 10, 18, 24, 49, 50, 51, 61, 62, 63, 65, 66, 67, 68, 69, 73, 74, 83, 98, 116, 118, 125, 129, 130, 133, 134, 159, 160, 162, 163

Trade Union, 24

Trotskyites, 46

War on Terror, 25

Warsi, Syeda, 94

Webb, Sydney and Beatrice, 41

Wilson, Harold, 43, 44, 82, 125, 128

women's rights, 14